Students, Schools, and Our Climate Moment

Students, Schools, and Our Climate Moment

Acting Now to Secure Our Future

LAURA A. SCHIFTER
WITH
JONATHAN KLEIN

Harvard Education Press
Cambridge, Massachusetts

Paperback ISBN 9781682539484

Library of Congress Cataloging-in-Publication Data is on file.

Published by Harvard Education Press,
an imprint of the Harvard Education Publishing Group

Harvard Education Press
8 Story Street
Cambridge, MA 02138

Cover Design: Endpaper Studio
Cover Image: Stacie Barton via Getty Images

The typefaces in this book are Carrara and Gotham.

For Ellie, Issie, and Thea
For Maya and Theo
To preserve a livable future,
For generations to come

CONTENTS

Introduction

> To care about climate change, we only have to be one thing: a human, living on planet earth.
>
> —Katharine Hayhoe[1]

Take a minute and consider the answer to this question: What motivates *you* to take action on climate change?

When each of us start conversations about the intersection of schools, education, and climate change, we start with this question. When people respond, they do not talk about degrees Celsius, polar bears on melting ice sheets, or technical or scientific issues. What we *do* hear is people discussing their children or people in their lives, their love of being outside, their connection to the local community or place.

When we have asked this question of the leaders we have worked with, they share a common response. For instance, former US Secretary of Education John B. King Jr. noted, "As an educator and the father of two daughters, I worry a lot about the world we are leaving our young people." Nikki Santos, former executive director for the Center for Native American Youth, remarked, "I can't imagine a future for my daughter where she doesn't have access and opportunities to connect to the land the same way I did because of climate change." Carlos Curbelo, former Republican member of the US House of Representatives from a district in the Miami-Dade area, said, "If I want my daughters to be able to have the choice to live in South Florida thirty, forty, fifty years from now, we're going to have to take action."[2] Despite coming from different backgrounds and different political perspectives, these leaders are united in action on climate to protect their children and future generations.

Whether you are concerned about the well-being of your children, health, the economy, national security, immigration, poverty, or safety, climate change impacts everyone and every sector of society. You may be concerned about being able to hike in the mountains, fish in a local stream, play at a park with your family, swim at the beach, cook your favorite meal, or drink a margarita—and climate change impacts them all. Climate change is a personal issue because it affects things that matter to us the most, and it affects things we love. It is easy, especially today, to focus on the things that divide us and get caught up in disagreements. To address climate change with the combined individual and collective action we need, we need to focus on what unites us. Studies confirm that this concern about "protecting the future for the next generation" is a unifying and motivating factor to take action on climate change not just nationally but around the globe.[3] And still there is much more we must do to center children and young people in solutions.

Despite the way many people talk about it, taking climate action is not simply trying to "save the planet." The truth is, regardless of what happens, the planet will continue to spin. What we are doing is trying to save the things we love, the things that bring us joy, and the things we care about. And we want to have these things preserved for future generations. Action on climate change is not just about saving the planet but about saving our ability, and the ability of future generations, to thrive on this planet. Plus, implementing solutions (modern, electric HVAC systems, sustainable schoolyards with shade, locally-sourced foods, education on climate, and more) makes an immediate, positive difference in the lives of our students and communities today.

In *Students, Schools, and Our Climate Moment,* we outline what it means to center children and young people in climate solutions and how educators and our K–12 schools can take comprehensive action. Our schools have the ability to drive tremendous change today and to invest in our future. Climate leaders Ayana Elizabeth Johnson and Katharine Wilkinson have emphasized the role committed individuals can play in advancing solutions by relying on their passions and strengths to pursue change.[4] We build on their work in this book to highlight the stories of people working in education. We underscore the opportunities to deploy climate solutions in schools and call attention to the personal narratives behind the individual drive to act, including our own.

LAURA'S CLIMATE JOURNEY

I was diagnosed with dyslexia when I was seven. At that time, my parents were told by specialists not to expect much from me academically. Fortunately, they didn't listen to the experts and held high expectations for my success. I was also extremely fortunate to have educators who held high expectations and provided me with the support I needed to reach those expectations. Because of the powerful impact educators had on my own experience, I developed a passion for education. I've had experience working as a first-grade teacher, an education researcher, a senior education policy adviser on the US House Committee on Education and Labor in Congress, and a graduate school lecturer. I work in education because I believe in its power to change lives and create opportunity. I know it did for me.

People change in a variety of ways; most often this change occurs over time. Sometimes the change occurs suddenly, where one day you are walking a path as one person, and the next your life is fundamentally altered. I've had three of those days in my own life. February 28, 2013, was the day my oldest daughter Ellie was born, and I was forever a different person as a mother. July 21, 2013, was the day we lost my twenty-eight-year-old brother-in-law, and I experienced the overwhelming weight of grief.

And October 8, 2018, when the United Nations Intergovernmental Panel on Climate Change (IPCC) released a report on the planet warming to 1.5°C.[5] My girls had a day off from school, and we were playing in the basement. I received news alert after news alert: we had just over a decade to address climate change and avoid the most devastating impacts. Frightened, I looked at my three children.

Before that moment, I had never thought of climate change as an issue that would be so pressing within my or my children's lifetimes. Although my husband, who had experienced his own climate reckoning years earlier, had been nagging me for years to care about climate change, climate had not been a top priority for me. It felt like something people working in the environmental movement were handling for the distant future, a problem for my children's children's children, maybe. And with it being so far away, I was sure technology would take care of everything. If someone had asked me if I knew what climate change was, I would have said I understood it, but if they asked me to explain it to someone else, I would have been lost immediately.

After Ellie was born, I, like many parents, flooded Instagram with photos of my baby. I decided to use the hashtag "#Ellie2056," 2056 being the year that Ellie would run for president. As I read the IPCC report that October day, what cycled through my head was a vision of the world Ellie would have to navigate as president. It was not some postapocalyptic water world but rather a world where climate refugees would push our global immigration system to the brink, where the strain on our resources would exacerbate poverty and increase international tensions and disputes, where equality and social justice would be impossible to achieve because of global instability, and where governments might be forced to impose oppressive restrictions on people's freedom to reduce societal emissions.

In one moment, all my feelings of motherhood and grief converged. I feared for my children's futures. I feared for their well-being. Despite the many pressing problems I had been working on in education, my previous work felt meaningless. We could have the best education system in the world, but it wouldn't matter if the full impacts of climate change took hold. This was my "climate moment."

Climate change became my top priority, and I realized very quickly how little I knew about it. I remember looking at my husband and saying, "Matt, oh my gosh, this is serious!" We looked at each other with a new understanding. I was on the other side of this issue now, the side where you visualize different scary futures in your head, the side where maybe you feel loss or paralysis by the scale and size of the issue. I felt all those things at once. Matt patted the couch and told me to sit down with him.

Action can be an antidote to despair. Since that moment (after my own stint of paralysis), I've tried to advance action. I looked into switching jobs and researched environmental organizations, but nothing felt right. In the spring of 2019, Washington State Governor Jay Inslee, in his presidential campaign, said on day one of his administration he would ask every federal department to submit its plan to address climate change. And I realized I did not have to enter a new field: I could bring my expertise in education to the climate fight.

Having worked in education policy for years, I recognized that we did not talk about climate change much in my field. At a systems level, the education sector had yet to mobilize at scale. And in conversations about advancing climate policy, people too often focused on technical solutions like solar or electric cars, but they underestimated the need to focus on education. I realized I might be able to bring people together to discuss the intersection more, and perhaps this group of people could draft a plan for the US Department of Education.

After I told my father about this idea, his initial response was, "Well, Laura, do you think there is something unique about what the education sector needs to do? Or does it just need to do what everyone needs to do on climate change?" I knew the answer was *yes,* there was something unique that education needed to do. And those of us within education needed to be the leaders of the charge.

I took a few days away from my family, and I attended a Climate Reality Project training in Atlanta, Georgia. I was blown away by the number of people there. Many of them were grappling with their own "climate moments" and searching for ways to make a difference. Through this training, I had the time and space to flesh out a plan and research the K–12 education sector's intersection with climate change.

After getting home from Atlanta, I started meeting with people who would introduce me to more people, who would introduce me to still more people. I learned there were amazing efforts being undertaken in pockets across the country. I remember speaking with Frank Niepold with the National Oceanic and Atmospheric Administration (NOAA), who had been working at the intersection of education and climate for years. I was worried he would be dismissive of a new effort, but I was relieved that minutes into talking he was enthusiastic and excited about the potential for new people coming to this work. There were also plenty of times when I spoke with people who didn't see the need or potential, or when I thought I wouldn't find another person to meet with to keep this idea moving forward.

I connected eventually with the Aspen Institute, a nonprofit organization committed to addressing our greatest societal challenges through dialogue, leadership, and action. Having worked on Capitol Hill in Washington, DC, I had known of the Aspen Institute and their work to support congressional staff as well as previous commissions that had successfully influenced policy. Steve Patrick, who led an effort called the Forum for Community Solutions, connected me with Greg Gershuny, who led the Aspen Institute's Energy and Environment Program. Greg agreed to help me launch K12 Climate Action, an initiative to unlock the power of the education sector to be a force for climate action, climate solutions, and environmental justice.

In February 2020, I felt like the initiative was moving toward success. Greg and I had been able to schedule a meeting for the end of March with former US Secretary of Education John King to discuss the idea. Just a few weeks later, that meeting switched to virtual as the world shut down for the COVID-19 pandemic, and my anxiety about the initiative's potential for success increased.

When we met virtually, however, I learned that King had grown increasingly concerned about climate change himself, and he recognized the need and the potential for the initiative. Christine Todd Whitman, a former administrator for the Environmental Protection Agency (EPA) and New Jersey governor, also acknowledged the critical opportunity to leverage the education sector in the climate fight and agreed to cochair the initiative.

With Whitman and King, we recruited twenty additional education, environment, civil rights, and youth climate leaders to join a commission to develop an action plan for the K–12 education sector. The commission included leaders like Becky Pringle, president of the National Education Association; Randi Weingarten, president of the American Federation of Teachers; Pedro Martinez, CEO of Chicago Public Schools; Debra Duardo, Los Angeles County Superintendent of Schools; and Pedro Rivera, former Secretary of Education for Pennsylvania. Later in this book, you'll meet several of the commissioners I had the privilege of working with: Naina Agrawal-Hardin, a climate activist and senior in high school when the commission started; Vic Barrett, a climate activist and plaintiff in the *Juliana et al. v. United States of America et al.* lawsuit; Kiera O'Brien, founder of Young Conservatives for Carbon Dividends; and Dr. Megan Bang, professor of learning sciences at Northwestern University.

This bipartisan commission recognized the urgent need to engage the education sector in advancing climate solutions. The commission held a listening tour to learn more about what the education sector needed to do and what was currently happening. It heard from students, educators, parents, and school leaders from across the country.

Looking for people to present before the K12 Climate Action Commission, I received many recommendations and spoke with leaders across the country, many of whom are featured in this book. When I first spoke with Maya Green, a recent high school graduate, she spoke passionately about the issues of race, inequity, and climate change in her hometown in Charleston, South Carolina. Gil Rosas, at the time energy manager with Stockton Unified, mentioned his role as a storyteller for his tribe, Cahuilla/Morongo Band of Mission Indians on his grandmother's side and Tejon Indian Tribe on his grandfather's side. He shared a video of Stockton's energy patrol—a group of elementary school students in yellow vests and hard hats—who patrolled schools helping educators understand energy-efficient strategies related to lights, plugging in electronics, and more. I spoke with Laura Capps, former school board member for Santa Barbara Unified School District, and Andie Madsen and Mahider Tadesse, former students in Salt Lake City Schools who were committed to advocating for change in their communities.

After this year of listening and learning, the commission released the K12 Climate Action Plan. This plan extends beyond simply a vision for the US Department of Education; it maps a comprehensive plan for America's K–12 education sector, including local school districts, state and federal policy makers, philanthropy, business, the media, and climate advocates. Through the plan, the commission envisioned a future where America's nearly 100,000 schools are beacons for climate action; where the 50 million students enrolled in schools are engaged in learning about our changing climate and solutions and are prepared for success in the clean economy; where schools are hubs for community resilience; where our buildings and 480,000 school buses run on clean renewable energy. In the subsequent chapters, we will build on this vision to help education leaders know how to make the recommendations from the plan actionable.

After the release of the K12 Climate Action Plan, we heard from many within the K–12 education sector who used this plan to advance action within their own communities. We also heard from those from early childhood, higher education, and children's media wanting to engage in similar efforts. As a result, we have rebranded our work as This Is Planet

Ed with the Aspen Institute, where "we believe children and youth will be essential in driving the urgent and lasting solutions we need, and we must empower them with knowledge and skills to advance a more sustainable, resilient, and equitable future."[6]

I started my journey as an anxious mother. For the past three years at our annual Aspen Ideas: Climate conference, we've hosted a dinner bringing together leaders working at this intersection. The first year, the dinner started as one table; the following year, it grew to a few tables; and this year, we needed to shift to our own private room. This issue is so large and there is so much that needs to be done that we must keep bringing more people to the table to work together for a brighter future for us, for all our children, and for future generations.

On my climate journey, the people I've been able to work with are what give me hope. Some of these new friends and colleagues have had their own climate moments well before I did; some had those moments after. We share a common commitment to action, to using our knowledge, passions, and positions to advance solutions.

Their stories inspire me and inspired us to write this book. I hope they will inspire you, too.

JONATHAN'S CLIMATE JOURNEY

When I finished college, my twenty-two-year-old self felt called to service to address the challenges facing marginalized students. I started as a fifth-grade teacher in Compton, south of Los Angeles, then moved to the Bay Area, where I had varied jobs over the years in education nonprofits, schools, and the Oakland Unified School District, most recently working as a leader of the California nonprofit committed to advocating for educational equity, GO Public Schools.

In the decade following the birth of my first child in 2007, I found myself taking screenshots of news headlines on my iPhone. The articles that called my attention covered weather events and scientific findings about the climate that seemed unusual compared to my past experiences. I often shared these headlines with family and friends, and after briefly expressing our concern, we would quickly move on with our days. We were all busy with our work, our children, our responsibilities and hopes. Earth's climate? The issue was too big and beyond our control. We hoped and assumed others were addressing it. For me, education was the main issue, and I was grateful for the opportunities to work toward solutions with parents, community leaders, educators, and elected officials over the years in that field.

In 2019, my forty-four-year-old self still felt deeply committed to rectifying the injustices within our public education systems and determined to see better opportunities and outcomes for the next generations of youth. I took a sabbatical, and with time to think, I connected the dots between my long-held intentions and a growing unease about climate change, which, as I came to recognize, had been simmering within me for years.

At that time, before the pandemic, our family in Northern California already kept N95 masks in our cars and backpacks. The wildfire and smoke season was becoming an unavoidable feature of California life, touching everyone, because of rising temperatures and persistent drought. Discussions with my wife, Amanda, often turned to worrying about plausible emergencies, to wondering how prepared we were, and to contemplating places we might move someday in light of changing weather patterns and climate conditions.

These outlier weather events began to suggest a distressing new normal for our world, and a new calling for me. I started to read. A college friend with experience in climate policy recommended I start with *The Uninhabitable Earth*, by David Wallace Wells, for its hard take on the truth, and *Drawdown*, by Paul Hawken, for its stance of defiant hope. Then I found Elizabeth Kolbert and Naomi Klein. Kim Stanley Robinson and Zoe Weil, and *The Overstory* by Richard Powers. I devoured books by these authors, eager to expand my understanding and discuss the issues with my family and friends.

In September 2019, my seventh-grade daughter invited me to chaperone her and her friends at a youth-led climate strike in San Francisco. That bright September day had a profound impact on me. I walked among thousands of passionate young people from diverse backgrounds, hearing their urgent, ambitious calls to action. I witnessed their anger, frustration, anxiety, and dread as they filled the streets of San Francisco on a school day, but also their clarity, as they pleaded with adults to acknowledge their responsibilities and the imperative for action to reshape priorities, habits, the economy . . . their lives. My daughter and her peers were frustrated that their schools were not adequately preparing them for the future. They were disillusioned by the indecision and inaction of adults from the baby boomer, Generation X, and millennial generations who hold formal authority. This crisis was unfolding on our watch, with their futures on the line. As I looked at their determined faces and read their protest signs, I imagined the challenges that awaited a classroom teacher in, let's say, 2029, after another decade of increasingly extreme weather had battered their homes, their schools, and human communities worldwide.

Questions raced through my mind: As a teacher, how would I engage and hold my students' attention? Would anything shape the lives of today's children more profoundly than rapidly changing climate and extreme weather? Would a liberal arts education, like mine, remain relevant? How would my students do their work, and what would they work on? How would they find their ways in life, to fall in love, to become parents?

I came to understand the injustices we are inflicting on younger and future generations. As the climate emergency has begun to unfold over the course of the professional lives of those in Generation X—*my* professional life—we have not made the necessary changes to prepare and educate our young people for a future that is being redefined by climate change. The purpose of education is to equip youth for the challenges of tomorrow, and by that fundamental measure, we were falling short.

I recognized that I was part of a generation of adults who have the authority, and therefore the responsibility, to respond to the call from young people for decisive action on climate. I thought about myself, my peers, and my friends, many of whom held leadership positions in nonprofit organizations, social enterprises, and corporate teams. Did I know *anyone* who was addressing climate change with the urgency and dedication that my daughter and other young protesters were demanding? Within days, I informed the board chair of GO Public Schools that I was ready for a transition and would be stepping down from my role leading the organization.

I had spent a long time in the world of public education, and as I prepared for my next move, I decided to start with what I knew best. I embarked on a mission to understand the intersections of educational equity and climate change. I began by talking to my contacts in the education sector about how climate change was impacting their leadership and priorities. Responses ranged from "It's not really a concern" to "I haven't thought about that," to "I should be doing more." These conversations could be difficult. I was showing up at meetings and events and going off-topic. I asked about the role of schools, teachers, and educational leaders in addressing climate change, while doing my best not to alienate people. With a smile, I started introducing myself as a "radicalized dad" or a "dadvocate."

Leaving a stable job and team I had built for an uncertain mission was intimidating. My twenty-two-year-old self had set my life on a path for which I am forever grateful, but my forty-four-year-old self was reevaluating the world and my role in it. I soon recognized that climate change was already having a profound impact on our students and educational opportunities. I learned that our school facilities are ill prepared to protect students from climate-driven threats like extreme heat and wildfire smoke. Our work for educational equity is being undone as climate change harms students' health, safety, and learning.

In the United States, I learned, millions of students are already losing valuable learning time each year because of extreme weather. Local economies are already being disrupted and are shifting, with some communities witnessing the disappearance of industries and jobs because of changing weather patterns. In these places, and in the many more still to come, K–12 schools need to collaborate with higher education and local businesses to envision new economic models and career pathways. It was the same infuriating story: long-standing, systemic inequities were still leaving schools that serve mostly Black and Brown, rural, Indigenous, and low-income children ill-equipped to handle extreme weather, making those children disproportionately vulnerable to the impacts of climate change.

Connecting with leaders and innovators in the green schools movement, I learned about schools that were leading the way in sustainability, resilience, and climate education. Concepts such as decarbonization and net zero became familiar. I saw the urgent need to shift perceptions of green schools from being merely an overlay on the standard design of a school facility to being the core of what education needs to be in light of the changing climate.

April 22, 2020, marked the world's fiftieth Earth Day, but it was the first one that truly resonated with me. I sat in our backyard, feeling the warmth of the late morning sun, a growing climate consciousness in my mind. And in my body, it turned out, the ongoing stirrings and discomfort of a long, persistent case of COVID-19. It was a moment of humbling vulnerability. This personal vulnerability along with our global vulnerability reminded me of the interdependence of all living things on Earth. We have a sacred and spiritual connection with each other, and to the planet, land, water, and other animals we are blessed to live among for the briefest of times.

My mind's eye turned toward the ways we live and work together. I saw how the pandemic had swiftly laid bare the inequity and fragility of our systems—health care, food, transportation, education, commercial supply chains. It was scary to me, to us adult generations, who came up in times of unprecedented prosperity and security. COVID-19 was humbling us. As an individual, I felt my mortality and prayed for the strength of the antibodies surging in my chest. As a parent, I was reminded of the uncertainty about the world ahead that we are passing on to our children. As a citizen and a voter, I considered the evidence of atrophy and insufficiency in our social safety nets, our resilience, and our basic capacity to care for each other.

I found myself smiling a little nonetheless. As I reflected, I was inspired by the speed, a matter of weeks, at which educators and families had reinvented schooling. The solutions were imperfect, of course, but everyone, from senior administrators to teachers and parents, was becoming more adaptable and questioning long-held assumptions about the twentieth-century school model. I envisioned how this spirit of urgent innovation could serve as a model for an effort to prioritize and activate K–12 schools in the battle for a livable climate future.

I was also reminded that the systems we rely on (demonstrably fragile and inequitable as they are) were designed and structured by people over generations, meaning they can be changed by people—by us—in the months and years ahead. I was reminded that "we can do hard things," as my children's teachers have often assured them when they need to tackle new subjects and difficult skills.

> **un·daunt·ed** (adjective): courageously resolute especially in the face of danger or difficulty : not discouraged[7]

I had been developing my ideas about climate and education in a Google document when a friend introduced me to Sara Ross, who had recently stepped back from her role as cofounder and CEO of a national residential solar financing company. It was immediately evident that Sara was deeply engaged in conceptualizing the powerful role that schools must play. Her insights and questions were invaluable, and our partnership (Sara with a climate policy and clean energy lens, me bringing knowledge and context about the education sector) became instrumental in shaping this new chapter in my work and leadership. Together with Jennifer Moses, who I knew from my time as an Aspen Pahara fellow, we launched UndauntedK12 in November 2020 on the day that I shared our ideas at the Clean Energy for Biden policy summit.

Later that month, as a "dadvocate" with a fledgling organization, I presented at a national workshop for school board members on climate and education, alongside Anisa Heming, executive director of the Center for Green Schools at the US Green Buildings Council. I'm forever grateful to Anisa for responding to a cold email and saying yes to engaging with me as a newcomer to her field.

As this book goes to press, it's 2024, and three plus years into our UndauntedK12 journey. We have engaged with generous, passionate, and capable partners across the country, and we are regularly sought after for advice and collaboration by federal and state agencies. We played a role in crafting the US Department of Education's new Climate Adaptation Plan. We are leading a national campaign to help America's public schools ensure healthy, resilient learning environments by leveraging tax credits and incentives through the federal Inflation Reduction Act to deploy clean energy technologies such as solar power and heat pumps.

I am clearer and more determined about this work than ever before. As we anticipated, three more years of storms and heat and smoke have driven more and more education leaders to the table with questions and a growing readiness for action. Each new year has reinforced the trend toward extreme weather disasters that do billions of dollars' worth of damage to homes, schools, businesses, and vital infrastructure.[8] Last year set new records for the hottest days ever recorded on Earth. The need for our response grows ever more urgent.

Still, my core idea is just the same as it was that day in San Francisco, when I began to walk beside my daughter and her friends. I am a parent, perhaps like you, determined to secure a better future for my children, grandchildren, and all future humans and living things on Earth. I'm also still an educator, still not quite and yet always becoming closer to an expert. I'm on a journey, one I never anticipated, and it's still not always comfortable. But I am learning how I can take meaningful action every day, and I believe that you can too.

ORGANIZATION OF THIS BOOK

After experiencing our climate moments, we learned, we were inspired by the passion and stories of people taking action, we partnered with others, and we developed plans to use our own strengths to drive change. Our experience with education is what we bring to the climate fight. We know this work can only be strengthened by others in education joining this fight as well. With this book, you will learn more about the intersection of climate change and education, opportunities for partnership, and avenues for action.

In chapter 1, we explore the motivations of those within the education sector and explain why everyone in education should care about climate change. We emphasize that it's urgent, that education will be key to solutions, and that there are benefits to education in doing this work. We share the experiences of students Kiera O'Brien, Vic Barrett, Naina Agrawal-Hardin, and Maya Green. They grew up attending school in different parts of the country during the 2010s as the impacts of climate change were accelerating in our communities, and yet they had little opportunity to learn about, understand, and process climate change in school.

In chapter 2, we build an understanding and awareness of key principles about climate change: that it's warming, it's us, it's here now, and we can advance solutions. We want those in education to feel confident in saying they understand climate change and that they can explain it to someone else.

Chapter 3 highlights the opportunity for the education sector to engage students in teaching and learning about climate change across the curriculum to build the knowledge and skills they need to thrive in a changing climate. We share the work of Dr. Megan Bang in Seattle Public

Schools in helping young students foster an understanding of our relationship to our environment, and former school board member Tammie Delaney in Hayden, Colorado, in creating sustainable career pathways for students.

In chapter 4, we discuss the opportunity for the education sector to advance solutions for schools to anticipate and adapt to a changing climate while supporting students' academic and mental health needs. We share the story of Miami-Dade Public Schools in their efforts to respond to Hurricane Maria, and the story of Laura Capps from Santa Barbara, California, who led an effort to adopt solar microgrids at schools to prepare the community for power outages.

Chapter 5 highlights the opportunity for the education sector to advance "mitigation solutions," or solutions to reduce the carbon pollution and emissions from schools. We share the stories of people across the country: Dr. Mike Hester former superintendent from Batesville, Arkansas, who led an initiative to adopt solar in the district; Gil Rosas, who has now led efforts in two districts to transition to electric school buses; and Janet Whited from San Diego, who has led an ambitious food waste reduction campaign.

In chapter 6, we emphasize the importance of collaboration across stakeholders, from school board members to students, educators to community members, to advance action. We discuss the opportunity for school leaders to leverage the Coherence Framework to develop comprehensive school district climate action plans to connect efforts across education, adaptation, and mitigation. We share the stories of Andie Madsen and Mahider Taddesse, who advocated for a school board resolution in Salt Lake City, and school board member Pamela Boozer-Strother, who led a collaborative climate action planning process in Prince George's County, Maryland.

In chapter 7, we connect the themes of the previous chapters and share actionable steps that you can take in your own community. We highlight what needs to shift in our schools and how different stakeholders (whether you are a parent or a school board member) can leverage their powers for action. Finally, we conclude by sharing messages of hope to leave you feeling empowered to take action in your own community.

Perhaps you are picking up this book because you've recently had your own climate moment, your students in your school have asked you questions, or maybe you have been working on this issue for years. Regardless of where you are, we need you. We hope, in offering this book, that climate change will become more of a priority for you, if it isn't already; that you will understand climate change, its causes, impacts, and solutions; that you will be inspired by the stories of others in this book; and that you will feel motivated and empowered to act in your own schools and community.

1

Why Should Schools Take Action on Climate Change?

***FIFTEEN-YEAR-OLD KIERA O'BRIEN** sat at her home in Ketchikan, Alaska, and looked out at the ocean, typically a deep blue. But on this day in late summer, it was a bright fluorescent blue. At first, she thought it was beautiful, but then it struck her that something was not right. Alaska was not the Caribbean; the water shouldn't look this way. The color was caused by an algal bloom that sucked all the oxygen out of the water. For the next several weeks, Kiera watched as dead fish washed up along the beach. This was her first memory, as she put it, "of something being profoundly off with the climate."*

At thirteen, Naina Agrawal-Hardin watched anxiously as the Gatlinburg fire raged near her maternal grandparents' house in east Tennessee, knowing just a slight shift in the wind could destroy the home where she had spent countless holidays and built deep family memories. Two years later, in Bihar, India, Naina's paternal grandparents' community experienced devastating monsoon flooding, while her other grandparents' community in Tennessee was still working to rebuild. It struck Naina that climate events were "not only happening in the present, but also leaving impacts that could be felt for years after their occurrence."

As a teenager in Charleston, South Carolina, Maya Green heard countless stories of people being trapped downtown when the roads flooded during high tides or rain. She recalled her mother purchasing a house and actively discussing the location of flood zones. A close friend's family relocated to Asheville, North Carolina, in search of higher ground. Each year in high school, at the start of school, Maya and her family were forced to pack their bags and evacuate their home for impending hurricanes. Maya recognized that climate change was having a "growing presence" in her own life.

Vic Barrett grew up as an Afro-Indigenous, Afro-Latino, and queer young person in upstate New York, where he felt an elevated level of concern for justice and fairness. As a teenager, Vic's family moved to New York City, where he had the opportunity to pursue his interest in human rights through an after-school program. Vic spoke to other students in the program who had lost their homes from Hurricane Sandy. Through those conversations, Vic realized that, to care about justice and fairness, he had to care about climate change. He realized that "climate change was a good thing to talk about if I wanted to talk about everything that mattered to people. . . . The climate is everything in so many ways."

No population has more at stake regarding climate change than today's young people. They are witnessing and experiencing the impacts of climate change directly, whether that's watching it on the news or seeing it in their backyards. They know these impacts will be here for decades and will only get worse.

At age eighteen, many millennials, Generation X members, and baby boomers took for granted that the Earth's climate would be stable. But an eighteen-year-old today faces a future clouded by limitations. Young people must ask themselves questions: Will I be able to live in a place I love ten years from now and feel safe? Should I have children? How will my job be shaped by climate change? Will climate change affect my health?

Young people in the United States and around the globe are increasingly concerned about climate change. In a 2021 survey, 75 percent of youth respondents indicated a moderate to extreme level of worry about climate change.[1] Many said that they felt "sad," "powerless," "anxious," "angry," and more. Even without directly experiencing the worst climate effects, witnessing climate impacts can lead to eco-anxiety—persistent worries about the future and the prospects for future generations.[2] This anxiety can fester when students aren't given ample opportunity to discuss climate change and learn about solutions and coping strategies to address these anxieties.

As many young people grapple with these issues, they see older generations stalling action while simultaneously heralding the younger generation as the people who will save our collective future. How can older generations expect young people to save the world when they don't see climate solutions and models for collective action in the places where they spend most of their time: their schools and communities?

We've had the privilege to work with amazing young people who have been grappling with the realities of climate change, working to process the issue, and advancing solutions. I (Laura) started K12 Climate Action with the Aspen Institute to develop an action plan for K–12 schools related to climate change, and I sought to ensure young people had a meaningful seat at the table. Kiera O'Brien, Naina Agrawal-Hardin, Vic Barrett, and Maya Green emerged as young leaders on issues related to climate, advocacy, and education. During my first conversations with them, I was amazed by their personal experiences as well as their commitment to these issues. Kiera recognized the importance of education, given that her parents were both public school teachers; Naina was poised and confident as a high schooler entering what might otherwise seem like an intimidating situation; Vic was excited about working on an issue he had advocated for years; and Maya shared her connection to her hometown, Charleston.

Kiera, Naina, Vic, and Maya all attended high school between 2012 and 2021, a period during which the impacts of climate change accelerated rapidly, alongside warnings from the global scientific community. Despite this increased urgency and living in different parts of the country, they all shared a common experience: they had insufficient or limited opportunities to learn about climate change in their own schools. Maya recalled that, despite this growing presence in her life and the life of her peers, climate change "was still so absent from my classrooms, and especially absent in a way that made it clear what I could do."

Why should schools care about climate change? We are asked this question a lot. There are many demands on education, and there are many pressing needs to deal with resource inequities, improve student performance, support student mental health, and more. It is hard to prioritize something that may not seem to have a big impact on the day-to-day work of teaching. However, climate change is already impacting educators' work. For students across the country, like Kiera, Naina, Vic, and Maya, it is impacting their lives. This impact will only become more pervasive.

There are four critical reasons why schools should care about taking action on climate change:

1. We have an urgent window for action.
2. Education is key to all climate solutions.
3. Climate action in schools is a win for education.
4. Education leaders owe it to students to act.

WE HAVE AN URGENT WINDOW FOR ACTION

For Naina, the void in education became most obvious after the 2016 presidential election. Naina was in middle school at the time and felt an increased sensitivity from her teachers about what could and couldn't be discussed in her classroom. The default perspective then from her teachers was: "We can't talk about that because we have to be fair to both sides, and so we're just not going to address the topic at all." It was shortly after the election that the Gatlinburg,

Tennessee, wildfire almost destroyed her grandparents' home, while simultaneously, President-elect Trump committed to pulling out of the Paris Agreement. Naina noted, "I felt this huge inconsistency between what I was feeling and experiencing at home and what was happening at school."

Naina's urgency to address climate change was accelerating rapidly with the impacts she witnessed in the communities she loved. She felt like we were "moving away from any action at all." These experiences heightened her own feelings of stress. "The more that the issue became politicized at the federal level, the less we talked about it in school."

When she did hear about climate change in school, it was presented in a way that was disconnected from human impacts and solutions. She would hear her teachers explain the greenhouse effect in her science class, but it always came with a disclaimer: "There's some debate among scientists about this theory." Naina said, "It just felt really, really inadequate."

Naina doesn't blame her teachers for the lack of conversation on climate change because she sensed many wanted to say more. "We would all sort of understand that there was more to be said on the topic. But it couldn't be talked about in that setting." She wished she had more opportunities to discuss the urgency of climate change with her teachers, noting, "I've taken a lot of general cues from educators about what questions are important [to ask] and how to make sense of the world around me."

Our global society and our ability to thrive depends on a stable climate. And yet we have put our climate on a path to instability. This instability is fundamentally reshaping our world, from how our schools operate to where children play, from decisions about jobs to where we live, from how we spend our free time to what we eat. Like Naina, students across the country feel and live this sense of urgency right now.

The United Nations has indicated that emissions reductions in this decade will determine our ability to limit warming to 1.5° or 2°C. To avoid the most devastating consequences, we must be on a path toward net-zero emissions by 2050, and currently, we are not on track to achieve these objectives.[3] Economist Spencer Glendon suggests that we have taken for granted an assumption of stability and now we must prepare ourselves for a series of "probable futures" living in an unstable climate—will it be instability at 1.5° warming, 2°, 2.5°, 3°, or more?[4] The degree of instability and associated climate effects depend on our actions today.

In many ways, these numbers may seem small, but each half degree Celsius comes with dire consequences. "A code red for humanity," "now or never," "sleepwalking to climate catastrophe," and "firmly on track to an unlivable world" are just some of the warnings UN Secretary-General António Guterres has emphasized year after year with each new UN report release on climate change.

The warnings of our "probable futures" go hand in hand with the realities of climate change we witness on the news, in our communities, and in our backyards: from excessive heat waves around the world, from California to Britain, to unprecedented flooding from Pakistan to Kentucky, to more intense wildfires, hurricanes, and droughts. Even if our existing emissions decrease immediately, a certain amount of warming is unavoidable. The questions now become: How much future warming can we avoid? And how can we adapt to live well in a changing climate?

Climate change is arguably the single greatest challenge humanity has faced. The scale and weight of the crisis can make it easy for people to lose hope and feel powerless. Those feelings are real. However, the window for action on climate change has not closed.

For decades, the UN has cataloged the research about climate change, but that research has failed to compel policy makers, businesses, and society to take action at the scale that we need. With the release of a 2022 UN report on climate change, UN Secretary-General Guterres said: "Young people, civil society and Indigenous communities are among those who have already stepped up, sounding the alarm and holding leaders accountable. We now need to build on their work to create a worldwide grass-roots movement that no one can ignore."[5] To build that grassroots movement, we need to bring people together. We need people—including those in education—to bring their interests, passions, and expertise to advance solutions.[6] Education is essential to building this movement, empowering people and communities, and unlocking solutions.

EDUCATION IS KEY TO ALL CLIMATE SOLUTIONS

Maya has a very vivid memory of her first conversation about climate change. She was on a trip visiting family in Barbados at about six or seven years old. One day, she was out on the water in a boat and her uncle, who worked in engineering, began explaining the greenhouse effect. She remembered him talking about the buildup of carbon dioxide in the atmosphere and how some carbon dioxide also gets absorbed into the ocean. He said it would make it "like Coca-Cola" and explained the impact it would have on ocean ecosystems and environments. That visual image stuck with Maya. She knew what Coca-Cola looked like—brown and bubbly—and how different that was from the water she saw sloshing around the boat that day.

Once she understood the greenhouse effect, Maya started looking for factors contributing to carbon dioxide in the atmosphere and for solutions. She remembers being in her bedroom and drawing a car with a plant to operate the engine rather than gas. Maya describes this first experience with climate as positive. "The fact that I had this conversation with my uncle, he took the time to explain it to me, and then I immediately started thinking about solutions." She added, "I've tried to hold on to that feeling in times where I've felt more hopeless and cynical as I've gotten older."

After that experience, Maya acknowledged a gap in conversations about climate change until high school. It had become more of a "household issue" after witnessing the effects of climate change on her community in Charleston. Yet it was not until she took AP Biology and, after that, AP Environmental Science, in eleventh grade that she learned about climate science in school. She described how these courses "broke down scientifically what was happening with climate change," and she "felt empowered by that knowledge." But she also added, despite discussing topics like nature, climate change was "totally absent from history, totally absent from other social sciences . . . and English." Maya felt an "absence of pathways in school . . . to do anything about what felt like a growing existential threat."

We have many technical solutions available to shift our systems toward sustainability. What we lack is the social and political will for transformative change. Education is a powerful lever to support social transformation. Researchers have acknowledged that education has been identified as a critical social tipping point to meet the societal decarbonization—the reduction in carbon use—needed by 2050 to help the world avoid the most devastating climate impacts.[7]

Too many people today have false ideas and misconceptions about climate change. This is partly the result of silence, misrepresentation, and equivocation about the issue in schools. These false ideas and misconceptions, which are perpetuated in schools, are a drag on and hindrance to action. In 2022, *Education Week* conducted a survey to probe teenagers' understanding about climate change.[8] While the vast majority of teenagers, nearly 80 percent, understand climate change to be real and primarily human-caused, they held key misunderstandings on the causes, consequences, and solutions. Forty-six percent of teens believed that the hole in the ozone layer was a major contributor to climate change; 27 percent believed the same about solar flares. Only 44 percent correctly understood that the greenhouse gas effect traps more heat in our atmosphere. Without a foundational understanding of the issue, how can we expect people to know what to do?

For Maya, learning about climate change at an early age helped her feel empowered to think about solutions. If humans are to address this most challenging of all challenges effectively, every young person must feel confident that they understand climate change—its causes; consequences; and, most critically, its solutions.

In addition to understanding the underlying science of the issue, we must also recognize that we need to restore our relationship with the natural world. We need to shift away from extractive mind-sets to acknowledging our interconnectedness with our environment. Indigenous communities around the world have not forgotten our critical relationship to our environment and our climate. This is probably the reason that, despite representing less than 5 percent of our global population, 80 percent of the world's remaining biodiversity is protected by Indigenous peoples.[9] With K12 Climate Action, I (Laura) have partnered with leaders from the Center for Native American Youth, including Nikki Santos (Coeur d'Alene Tribe) and Owen Oliver (Quinault/Isleta Pueblo) to ensure Indigenous perspectives are meaningfully reflected in our call to action for schools. At the inaugural Aspen Ideas: Climate in Miami Beach in 2022, Nikki and Owen gave a powerful speech about rebuilding our relationship with nature. They emphasized that we all must remember the teachings of Chief Seattle, a famous Suquamish and Duwamish chief: "This we know: The Earth does not belong to man, man belongs to the Earth. All things are connected like the blood that unites us all. Man did not weave the web of life. He is merely a strand in it. Whatever he does to the web, he does to himself."

Somehow that understanding—that we depend on our climate to live our lives the way we do—has disappeared for many in our global society. This understanding is something that we must rebuild. People, not simply technology, will help us all emerge from and persist through this crisis, but we need to support people—to break our assumptions of stability, develop our understanding, and build our capacity to act. We need education to step up.

CLIMATE ACTION IN SCHOOLS IS A WIN FOR EDUCATION

In science class, Vic remembers learning about concepts like the ozone layer and "seeing lots of photos of polar bears." Although the science of climate change may have been discussed in relation to these photos, he didn't deeply engage. The photos of polar bears were disconnected from the issues Vic cared most about—human rights, justice, and equality.

When Vic's family moved to New York City, Vic became excited to learn about the United Nations. "I thought the UN was the coolest thing ever." His freshman class took a field trip to the UN, deepening Vic's interest. "I was obsessed with learning about the Declaration of Human Rights." Even though Vic's history teacher did not explicitly teach about climate change, the teacher did encourage students to get involved in out-of-school activities. The afterschool program Global Kids visited Vic's ninth-grade history class. After learning about their program, Vic signed up, and through this program, Vic met peers who had lost their homes in Hurricane Sandy. According to Vic, his exposure to climate education and advocacy, just "all snowballed from there."

Also through this work, Vic understood that, to advance equity and justice, he would need to address climate change. Grappling with climate change through an intersectional lens and seeing how it impacted people (outside the science classroom) engaged Vic. It made learning relevant to his interests, concerns, and life.

The issue of climate change does not exist in isolation. It is an underlying issue that is connected to many subjects that educators care about: health, the economy, equity, and more. Just as the impacts of climate change exacerbate problems across a variety of issues, climate solutions also have cross-cutting benefits. Educators can use this moment to advance equity; access funding, resources, and support; and create healthy sustainable learning spaces where children and youth thrive.

For decades, educators have sought to advance equity, recognizing the role that education plays in creating a pathway to opportunity for all children and youth, regardless of their zip code. Yet Black, Latino, Indigenous, and other students of color; low-income rural and urban students; and students with disabilities have not been afforded equitable educational opportunities at scale, and gaps in academic achievement and graduation outcomes persist. For instance, state and local revenue for education is lower in districts with higher proportions of students of color (as much as $2,700 less per student) than districts with lower proportions of students of color.[10]

This inequity in education builds on broader systemic inequity, which has created barriers for Black, Latino, Indigenous, and other children of color; low-income rural and urban children; and children with disabilities from achieving success. For instance, redlining, a practice that originated with the Federal House Administration during the New Deal in the 1930s, discouraged banks from providing mortgages to people located in areas with large populations of Black residents. This policy increased economic inequity, prevented families from building wealth, and encouraged segregation.[11] As a consequence of these policies promoting racial segregation, children of color and Indigenous children still disproportionately live in areas where they are exposed to more air pollution today, resulting in higher rates of asthma. Asthma rates among Black children are more than double the rate for white children, 12.3 percent compared to 5.5 percent.[12] These systemic injustices have a direct impact on students' abilities to attend, learn in, and succeed in school.

Climate change will further exacerbate these existing inequities. Air pollution, heat, and extreme weather will have a greater impact on student learning, particularly for students of color, Indigenous students, and students from low-income rural and urban communities. Schools in communities of color with higher populations of lower-income students have less access to infrastructure funding for maintenance, meaning that they are less able to keep students safe, comfortable, and learning, for instance, because they frequently close on hot days. Schools with higher populations of low-income students experience the most damage from extreme weather and have the hardest time recovering.[13]

These effects will only widen gaps as climate change worsens unless we take action to prevent it. Equity-centered action on climate change is necessary to help educators counter the unequal impact of climate change on schools. Rather than waiting to respond to the effects, educators can anticipate these inequities and address them head on.

Solutions for schools, such as installing solar microgrids, can help communities be more responsive to extreme weather. They can be leveraged as hubs of resilience where historic divestment has prevented communities from being prepared for extreme weather. Sustainable schoolyards that rely on native landscapes rather than heat-trapping asphalt can reduce heat and pollution at the school and in the surrounding community while simultaneously increasing access to green space and improving opportunities to learn.

The following chapters will lay out these solutions and show that they can also help reduce funding inequities. Supporting under-resourced schools by investing in infrastructure improvements to reduce energy demand and increase the use of renewable energy means reductions in schools' annual operating budgets, and these funds can be reinvested directly into the teaching and learning in schools.

Focusing on these solutions is also an opportunity to ensure that our places of learning are healthy, sustainable environments where children can thrive. Reducing pollution associated with the burning of fossil fuels—whether directly in the building from fossil-fuel-dependent systems or in the neighborhood from buses with diesel tailpipe emissions—creates healthier spaces for children to learn and educators to teach.

Advancing climate solutions requires community buy-in, awareness, resources, and more. The benefits are worth it. Throughout our conversations with educators, we consistently hear how taking action was easier than they thought it would be when the community realized the tremendous benefits. Taking action on climate change in schools is a win for education.

EDUCATION LEADERS OWE IT TO STUDENTS TO ACT

Being born and raised in Ketchikan, Alaska, Kiera's childhood was "outdoorsy." Her parents had been park rangers in Yosemite National Park and Glacier National Park before becoming public school educators. For Kiera and her sisters, living in Alaska meant that they grew up attuned to the "cycles of nature." She knew Ketchikan could expect about thirteen feet of rain every year and that October would be brutally cold with wind and rain whipping everywhere.[14] *She knew the ins and outs of deer and fishing season. About her childhood, Kiera said: "You're just kind of free to roam when you are a kid in Alaska. . . . It's like, if you're having a bad day, you go for a walk in the woods." Kiera acknowledged that growing up in Alaska meant that "it's kind of impossible to ignore the natural world around you."*

Despite this proximity to the natural world, Kiera's school did not discuss climate change. "For me, I wasn't exposed to the concept of climate change, not through school anyway, until college." As the fastest-warming state in the United States, Kiera described Alaska "as the ground zero of climate change." Even though it was not taught in school, Kiera said, "Of course you notice changes as they happen."

After seeing the algal bloom outside her family's home, Kiera wanted to know what could make something like that happen. Her father, a biology teacher, explained to her the science behind the algal bloom, but still she wanted to know more. With the silence at school on these topics, Kiera searched for answers online.

With the impacts of climate change intensifying, children and youth, especially those from historically underserved communities, will experience these impacts the most despite being the least responsible for them. Climate change will have a significant impact on their health, well-being, learning, security, and economic prospects. Education leaders have a responsibility to face this reality head on. They can do this by taking action, modeling solutions, and adapting to climate impacts. It is important that they begin by talking about it.

Growing up in the 1980s and 1990s, Jonathan and I learned very little in school about climate change, its impacts, its consequences, and its solutions. Decades later, according to a survey by the Washington Post/Kaiser Family Foundation in 2019, this had not significantly changed—only 15 percent of teenagers (ages thirteen to seventeen) indicated they knew "a lot" about how to reduce the effects of climate change, and only 14 percent said they learned a lot about reducing the impact of climate change in school.[15]

For too long, our schools have been silent on climate change. Kiera, Vic, Naina, and Maya expected to find answers and discussion in their schools, but that did not happen. Kiera hopes school today will foster "an environment where students feel comfortable talking to each other about what they're seeing, what they're experiencing, what they think the issues and answers are because in so many settings that's very prescriptive." There is an opportunity to "allow for student experiences, for people to contribute new ideas" and to appreciate that "their own personal experiences [are] a value."

Vic wants schools to talk about climate change in a way that doesn't restrict it to the science classroom. Vic feels that the way climate is taught now is "very surface level," but hopes it can be connected to the "full big picture. . . . It's not about things that are just outside of you. It's about things that are everyday." We need to "understand the impact it has on humans." He added, "We don't want to make people feel hopeless, but I just wish I learned more about it. I wouldn't have felt hopeless if I learned more about what I could do."

Maya wished that adults at schools would end the silence, even if they don't have all the solutions. "Even just the institutions around me admitting that this is a problem and that they wanted to work with me on solutions would have been leagues better than ignoring it." She added, "No one is expecting adults to have all of the solutions." But she would like to see adults admit that "this is a problem that will be really pressing for your generation and will disproportionately impact marginalized communities. And we're committed to thinking about solutions with you." Where Maya had felt her concerns weren't validated, she thought this approach "would have been so affirming."

Like Maya, Naina also recognized that creating meaningful rather than superficial dialogue in school would help reaffirm her own concerns. She kept questioning herself, wondering, "Am I too worried about this?" The absence of meaningful dialogue "almost felt like gaslighting" because she was "so concerned" about a topic that was broadly overlooked by our education system. Finding that community for herself is also what she hopes for others, "being validated—your fear for the future and your hope about what collective action could accomplish—in the face of the climate crisis, was a huge release."

Fortunately, we are starting to move in the right direction. In 2020, New Jersey became the first state in the country to pass cross-curricular climate change standards.[16] First Lady of New Jersey Tammy Snyder Murphy worked with educators across the state to advance these standards. In discussing this accomplishment, Murphy noted:

> New Jersey's educational system became the first public school system to admit that climate change is a real, tangible problem that this generation of children will be required to face, and further, that it is our duty to prepare them for that certain future. By including climate change education across all core subjects from Kindergarten through high school graduation, every New Jersey student will be prepared to explore, imagine, and advocate for the innovative solutions needed in the communities in which they live.[17]

Talking about climate change and teaching it are critical first steps. We need school systems across the country to follow New Jersey's lead by starting conversations and creating space for students to grapple with climate challenges and engage with solutions. This movement is gaining traction globally: in the same year that New Jersey enacted this policy, Italy mandated climate education for its students.[18] However, this is just one step in education leaders meeting our responsibility to students. Education leaders also must fulfill their responsibility to create a more sustainable, adaptable, resilient, and equitable society to put us on a better track. They can create systems of learning prepared to withstand climate impacts, reduce our schools' reliance on fossil fuels and stop contributing to the warming of the planet, and partner with students to advance action.

A VISION FOR THE FUTURE

> [We need to] let go of the history we've had of not caring for each other, and especially as a young Black person, a young Indigenous person in the United States, even when I imagine a world with no fossil fuels, I'm imagining a world that cares about me as well.
>
> —Vic

In early June 2023, as students and schools across the country were preparing for end-of-year school celebrations—class picnics, field days, and graduations—wildfire smoke from Canada engulfed much of the US East Coast. Air quality in the Washington, DC, area was classified as "unhealthy"; air quality in New York was "hazardous."[19] The sky appeared a hazy orange, obscuring views of the Brooklyn Bridge in New York, the Capitol in Washington, and more. The smell of smoke sat in the air. Schools were forced to keep children inside to avoid having them breathe in polluted air.[20] After years of wearing masks indoors because of COVID, many children now needed them outdoors too. Wildfire smoke, which carries toxic fine particles in particular, is ten times more harmful to children's health than other forms of pollution.[21] Black and Latino children, who are disproportionately exposed to air pollution, were particularly susceptible to health impacts, including asthma-related emergency room visits.[22] This reality for the East Coast is something students in the western part of the country have grappled with for years.[23] The 2023 Canadian wildfires, the worst season on record, continued to burn, sending waves of smoke over cities from Chicago to Milwaukee, to Detroit. Canada had experienced significant drought and heat—both effects of climate change—which spurred the out-of-control fire season.

Try to imagine how much different our global position might be today if twenty years ago, we had made the investments in our schools to support teaching and learning about climate change. What if our schools had integrated climate solutions into students' experiences and helped students develop sustainable mind-sets? How might our political leaders, business leaders, and communities be different today? Perhaps there might be a broader consensus for action, perhaps there might be clarity on how all people might contribute, and perhaps we might have bent the curve further to decrease our emissions to stay below a 1.5°C warming threshold, thus avoiding the polluted air, school closures, and other climate impacts we are living with now.

With 100,000 schools educating 50 million students (one in every six Americans) across this country, our schools offer tremendous opportunity for making a difference. Schools are located in every community. Leveraging schools as assets in the fight against climate change can help us build resilience, decrease emissions from a large public sector, and empower the youngest generation for success.

To borrow an old cliché, it is true that the best time to have planted this tree may have been twenty years ago (or earlier), but the second-best time to plant a tree is today. We like to imagine twenty years from now not as a climate apocalyptic disaster but rather a sustainable, adaptable, and equitable society, where students can breathe clean air, step onto a zero-emission electric school bus, and attend a school where lights are powered from the sun and the buildings are heated and cooled with geothermal energy. The schoolyards would be green, sustainable learning spaces, and lunches would consist of locally grown, sustainable food. School districts would reap the savings from lower energy bills. Climate impacts would still occur, but we would be prepared to respond to them. Schools would have safe indoor air quality when there is worse outdoor air quality and access to clean air, all of which would not be dictated by the color of students' skin. All community members would have safe spaces to go in extreme weather, and students would have the social emotional supports they need to build resilience and thrive. A future where, upon graduation, students would be prepared to lead and succeed in a robust, clean, sustainable, and equitable economy. It won't be easy to get to that future.

Education remains an underutilized asset in the climate fight. Tapping into the power of education to model solutions, foster resilience, and empower young people with the needed knowledge, skills, and mind-sets can help build a brighter future. Building that future depends on us all now working together, learning, and committing to act. Why should schools act on climate change? We have to, and we hope the stories of the people in the chapters that follow can help you on your journey to action.

Key Takeaways

1. *We have an urgent window for action*: Action on climate change over the next decade is essential to avoid its most devastating impacts.
2. *Education is key to all climate solutions*: Empowering people with the knowledge and skills to advance solutions—leveraging their strengths, interests, and passions—will help catalyze the action we need at scale.
3. *Climate action in schools is a win for education*: Accelerating solutions on climate change has intersectional benefits with other educational priorities—advancing equity, increasing resources for teaching and learning, engaging students, and improving learning conditions, to name a few.
4. *Education leaders owe it to students to act*: Young people crave leadership on climate change. Through action and collaboration, education leaders can demonstrate to young people that they care about their students' future.

2

What Is Climate Change and What Can We Do?

LAURA'S REFLECTION: *After experiencing my own climate moment, one of the first things I knew I needed to do was learn. I needed to understand what climate change was and what we could do about it. Before having my climate moment, I had not been oblivious to climate change. I knew it was a problem. I just did not think it was one that I fully needed to understand. I took comfort in the myth that it was an issue being handled by environmentalists and not an issue that would likely impact me in my lifetime or my children in their lifetimes. Perhaps it would be a problem for my grandchildren's children, but by then technology would surely have taken care of it.*

I thought I understood the issue—I didn't deny climate change existed, but if someone had asked me to explain it to them, I would not have been able to, or the explanation would have been rooted in the myths that I believed. After my climate moment, that changed. I needed to learn about climate change. I needed to be confident enough in my understanding that I could explain it to someone else. When I teach now, I typically ask my students through an anonymous poll in the first class, "How well do you understand climate change?" The potential responses include "Not at all," "Sort of," "Understand it," or "Understand it and can explain it to someone else." Through this exercise, I find there are many others who feel they understand it, but they do not understand it at a level where they think they can explain it to someone else. This needs to shift if we are going to take on climate action at scale.

Scientists have long understood the dangerous effects of climate change, and yet they have faced hurdles in motivating change. This is unsurprising because many people hold misconceptions about the issue, and it is often portrayed as being too complex for most people to understand. While there are incredible complexities to climate change, climate communications leaders, among others, have highlighted the simple core concepts we all need to understand. The Yale Program on Climate Change Communication (YPCCC) seeks to articulate these core concepts through "five facts, ten words."

1. It's real;
2. It's us;
3. It's bad;
4. Scientists agree . . .
5. . . . there's hope![1]

In this chapter, we discuss these key understandings and describe how educators can think about the solutions, specifically, what climate mitigation and adaptation mean for education, the unique role of education in advancing solutions, and the opportunity through this work to advance equity for the communities most affected by climate and educational injustice. Many may feel they already have a sufficient grasp on climate change: its causes, consequences, and solutions. Our objective in the following sections is to provide a foundational understanding of climate basics and provide metaphors, examples, and analogies to help support additional conversations on climate change and the role of education.

IT'S REAL. IT'S WARMING. WHAT IS CLIMATE CHANGE?

Laura's reflection: When my daughter was in second grade, she came home from school and told me we live on the "Goldilocks" planet. This term was not something I had previously heard. She explained further. Earth is not too hot, not too cold—it is the "just right" planet to sustain life.

This notion of the Goldilocks planet is the first and most important thing to understand about climate change. The climate conditions of our planet enable us to live and thrive, and humanity thrives because those conditions are "just right."

One of the key features that makes Earth a "just right" planet is our atmosphere, the layer of gases surrounding the planet. Our atmosphere acts as a heat-trapping blanket around the Earth to create stable temperature ranges that allow us to live, grow food, access water, and thrive. Just like a sheet versus a thick comforter matters in keeping one warm at night, the material of our heat-trapping blanket matters as well. Greenhouse gases (for example, carbon dioxide and methane) at the right levels help us maintain predictable and stable climates by trapping the heat from the sun's radiation within the atmosphere while also allowing some of the heat to escape. This is known as the greenhouse gas effect.

Other planets do not benefit from that stability because of the composition of their atmospheres. For example, the atmosphere on Mercury is very thin, with very few greenhouse gases. Mercury's atmosphere does not have the ability to maintain and moderate its climate. When one side of Mercury is facing the sun, it gets dramatically hotter; the side away from the sun gets dramatically colder. Venus, on the other hand, has an atmosphere filled with greenhouse gases. The greenhouse gas effect on Venus is so powerful that it is the hottest planet in the solar system, despite being further away from the sun than Mercury.

For about six thousand years before the industrial revolution, carbon dioxide levels in the atmosphere on Earth hovered consistently at about

280 parts per million.[2] With this level, the amount of heat trapped by the atmosphere created a stable and predictable range of temperatures on Earth. This predictability enabled humans to shift from being nomads to being farmers. It allowed groups to settle; to create towns, communities, and cities; and to form large societies.

Since the industrial revolution, we have been changing the material of our gas blanket. Driven in large part by the burning of fossil fuels, we have emitted more heat-trapping greenhouse gases, or carbon pollution, into the atmosphere. As a result, we have increased the average global temperature of the planet. It's like changing from a light quilt to a heavy comforter. The current levels of carbon dioxide in the atmosphere measure at about 420 parts per million.[3] The last time the Earth's carbon dioxide levels were that high was over 4 million years ago. The Earth's average temperature was about 3° to 4°C warmer than it is today; sea levels were anywhere from 16 to more than 130 feet higher than today.[4]

The UN's Intergovernmental Panel on Climate Change (IPCC), consisting of scientists around the world, has made it clear that to avoid the most devastating effects of climate change, our world needs to decrease our carbon pollution or emissions rapidly, and we need to make significant progress in the next decade. In the 2023 report from the IPCC, scientists concluded that current human activities related to carbon pollution have "unequivocally" resulted in global warming.[5] This has already resulted in an average increase of global mean surface temperature of 1.1°C over preindustrial levels and will likely hit 1.5° in the coming decades. In the United States, where we tend not to think of temperature in °C, 1.5° warming equates to about 2.7°F. According to the IPCC climate models, 1.5°C warming is likely, and regardless of actions today, we will feel significant effects related to this level of warming for decades to come. Action in the next decade is critical to help us avoid warming of 2°C or higher. Half a degree of difference may not seem like a large distinction to many, but the projected consequences are significant: more exposure to extreme heat, an increase in the number and the severity of droughts, species loss, food insecurity, worsening health, and economic loss.[6] These impacts interact with and compound each other. They have the potential to create climate "tipping points," where damage becomes irreversible and self-perpetuating. These cascading possibilities have devastating impacts for humanity and our ability to adapt.[7]

The scientific consensus is clear—we are experiencing global warming. Global warming is changing our climate. We need to reduce the warming to the greatest extent possible and adapt to living on a warming planet.

IT'S US. WHAT ARE THE MAIN DRIVERS OF CLIMATE CHANGE?

In the early 2000s, scientists began to suggest that we are living in a new geological period called the Anthropocene. This new geologic period is defined by human activity altering the Earth's climate and the environment.[8]

Since the 1800s, the industrial revolution and human activity since then have fundamentally changed our society. Technological advances in energy production, transportation, manufacturing, and more put our society and economy on a new path. Today, we no longer rely on horse-drawn carriages to travel or wood-burning fires to heat our homes. New technologies have also enabled exponential population growth, putting more pressure on the Earth's natural resources.[9] Much of our daily lives depend in part on the burning of fossil fuels, which emits carbon pollution into our atmosphere. Overall, carbon dioxide accounts for the largest proportion of greenhouse gas emissions (76 percent globally, 79 percent in the United States). Methane emissions (18 percent globally, 11 percent in the United States), nitrous oxide, and fluorinated gases constitute the remaining human-generated emissions.[10]

While many human factors have a direct impact on greenhouse gases (like gas-powered cars or coal-fired power plants), there are also "sinks" that can absorb greenhouse gas emissions. Sinks can be naturally occurring—trees and the ocean are two examples—or human-created newer technologies such as carbon sequestration. Human activities that increase direct emissions and decrease naturally absorbing sinks (like deforestation) lead to a net increase of greenhouse gases in the atmosphere.

While many countries contribute to the Earth's global emissions, the United States has cumulatively been the largest contributor.[11] The industrial revolution propelled the US economy and its standing in the world as we rapidly expanded transportation, electricity, and manufacturing. Today, we burn fossil fuels when we drive gas-powered cars and when we rely on coal-fired power plants or natural gas for our electricity. We burn fossil fuels to heat and cool our homes and when we make things. For agriculture, we make decisions about managing soil that releases emissions. Livestock can also emit methane—a particularly potent greenhouse gas. In the United States, the following sectors account for our domestic emissions: transportation (28 percent), electricity (25 percent), industry (23 percent), residential and commercial buildings (13 percent), and agriculture (10 percent).[12] Given our role in causing this problem, we bear significant responsibility in fixing it. We need to rethink and shift our current practices across these sectors.

Decisions around land use can either be positive, when they preserve the capacity to absorb emissions, or negative, when carbon-sinking forests are removed or destroyed. Since the industrial revolution and colonization, the culture of extraction, with little focus on preservation and conservation, has led to a significant reduction in naturally absorbing carbon sinks and to unjust and inequitable outcomes for people. The 2022 IPCC report on adaptation recognized that "vulnerability of ecosystems and people to climate change differs substantially among and within regions, driven by patterns of intersecting socio-economic development, unsustainable ocean and land use, inequity, marginalization, historical and ongoing patterns of inequity such as colonialism, and governance."[13] In particular, the forced displacement of Indigenous peoples who managed land corresponded with clearing of forests and natural habitats. These intersectional issues continue to threaten progress today.

The way we have grown accustomed to our lives and the policies, structures, and systems connected to this current way of life—from our energy use, transportation, buildings, manufacturing, food production, and land use—are driving climate change. And this human-caused climate change is impacting us now.

IT'S BAD. WHAT ARE THE MAIN IMPACTS OF CLIMATE CHANGE?

Laura's reflection: On July 13, 2023, I received a Washington Post *news alert on my phone: "Flooding, extreme heat waves, and hot oceans will continue—and get worse."*[14] *The day before, I emailed a colleague living in Vermont, and I hesitated thinking about the images I'd seen of catastrophic flooding. I did not know if this colleague's home had been flooded or if his family and loved ones were safe. Later I was on a Zoom meeting with people from Miami Beach who said that the ocean water there felt like entering a hot tub, and they expressed concerns about what it meant for the ocean's wildlife. Meanwhile, 108 million Americans were living under a heat alert advisory. Temperatures in parts of the Southwest were expected to approach 130°F.*[15] *This was all in two days of summer 2023.*

It's increasingly hard to ignore the pervasive and unrelenting moments of extreme weather. Yet it is hard to absorb the full impact of climate change. Shifts in average patterns of weather take place over a longer period and can be more difficult to perceive, leading to misconceptions. Weather is what we experience daily when we walk out the front door and decide if we need a coat, a hat, sunglasses, or an umbrella. Climate is the average of our daily weather patterns, and climate change is the shift in those averages. People may assume that climate change is less significant because tomorrow's weather forecast is for a cold day. Or they may treat climate effects as typical because one storm in the distant past reached a similar level of destruction. But it is not the individual weather events that represent climate change but the changes in the average weather patterns over time.[16] These changes in averages are destabilizing our climate and leading to more frequent and more severe destruction.

In 2023, the US Environmental Protection Agency (EPA) released *Climate Change and Children's Health and Well-Being*, documenting the extensive effects that heat, air pollution, flooding, and infectious disease will have on children.[17] The report acknowledges, "Children, and young children especially, have less control over their physical environments, less knowledge about health effects from climate change, and less ability to remove themselves from harm. Climate impacts experienced during childhood can have lifelong consequences stemming from effects on learning, physical development, chronic disease, or other complications."

This book emphasizes hope and our collective potential to take action to address the global existential crisis we face. However, it would be a disservice to the climate crisis not to emphasize what is at stake, not just for future generations but for us today.

Impact on Extreme Weather

Hot spells are hotter. Droughts are more intense. Storms are more dangerous. This, in turn, leads to sea level rise, loss of species, food insecurity, increased poverty, climate migration, worsening health, and loss of life.

According to the World Meteorological Organization in January 2023, the eight years from 2015 through 2022 were the eight warmest years for the world on record.[18] The year 2023 then broke through all previous records to become the hottest year ever recorded.[19] With higher average temperatures, the United States is experiencing more frequent and longer heat waves. Looking at data across fifty US cities, the EPA noted that the heat wave season is now forty-six days longer on average than it was in the 1960s, and the average number of heat waves have jumped from two to six during that time period.[20] The IPCC summed up their findings on impacts and adaptation with "high confidence" as follows: "The rise in weather and climate extremes has led to some irreversible impacts as natural and human systems are pushed beyond their ability to adapt."[21]

This extreme weather plagued the start of the 2022–2023 school year. In July 2022, in eastern Kentucky, heavy rainfall caused historic flooding. This flooding impacted twenty-five school districts, with some delaying their school opening for several weeks.[22] A weeklong oppressive heat wave in California had temperatures in Sacramento reach 116°F.[23] Schools with insufficient air conditioning were forced to send children home early.[24] At the end of September 2022, Hurricane Ian tore through Florida, leaving schools devastated in its aftermath. Some schools were closed for months.[25]

In August 2022, Jackson, Mississippi, saw heavy rainfall followed by significant flooding. The floods overwhelmed the city's water treatment plants, forcing schools to shift to remote learning at the start of the year.[26] Underinvestment in the city's water and school infrastructure buckled when faced with what is becoming increasingly more common: heavy rain and floods. These climate impacts further exacerbated existing inequities. In addition to being unable to drink the brown mucky water, children were unable to flush toilets. In making the decision to close schools and shift to remote learning, Dr. Errick Greene, superintendent of Jackson Public Schools told National Public Radio (NPR), "This right here, it's almost unbelievable. If I weren't living it and talking about it all freaking day, almost unbelievable."[27]

The COVID-19 pandemic highlighted across the country how sensitive our students, families, and communities are to school disruptions and closures. Although we have yet to understand the full impacts of the pandemic on children and youth, we have seen declines in National Assessment of Educational Progress (NAEP) scores, heightened anxiety, isolation, and missing and disengaged students.[28] Climate change is also closing and disrupting schools across the country, and this disruption will increase as climate effects accelerate. By the time this book is published, there will be numerous additional examples of extreme hot days, floods, wildfires, and hurricanes that have closed schools.

Impact on Health

The impacts of climate change on children's health begin as early as pregnancy and continue through early development. Exposure to heat and air pollution is associated with increased prevalence of low birthweight, preterm birth, and stillbirth, especially for Black mothers.[29] Wildfire smoke in particular has been found to permeate the placenta, having a direct impact on fetal development.[30] Preterm birth and low birthweight are associated with an increased risk of children developing disabilities, health conditions, and social and learning challenges.[31]

Climate change can be dangerous for children's health because of their ongoing physical and behavioral development, including an increased prevalence of childhood asthma and allergies.[32] Over 4 million children and youth under age eighteen currently have asthma, with Black children being twice as likely as white children to be diagnosed.[33] Higher temperatures have increased pollen counts, and researchers have found that our allergy season is already twenty days longer than it was in 1990.[34] Hot days, increased pollen, and poor air quality can exacerbate respiratory illness and asthma attacks, and students with asthma are more likely to miss school.[35] Children, in particular those with chronic health conditions such as asthma or diabetes, are more susceptible to heat-related illnesses, including heat stroke and dehydration.[36]

Extreme weather, including heat, droughts, and flooding, as in Jackson, Mississippi, impact the availability of safe and healthy food and water, and further affect children's brain development.[37] The health risks related to the impacts of climate change on water quality, air quality, and food access are particularly high for Indigenous children and communities in both urban and rural settings.[38] Climate effects will also directly expose students to trauma and adverse childhood experiences. More intense floods, wildfires, and hurricanes bring with them increased loss of life, homes, and livelihoods. Children and youth are especially vulnerable to the impacts of trauma and uncertainty that they, without support and intervention, may carry with them into adulthood.[39]

Impact on Student Learning

Student learning is being and will increasingly be affected by school closures, physical health impacts, and mental health impacts. Heat itself hurts student's ability to learn. Research has shown that exposure to high heat, in addition to the added health risk, has substantial effects on student learning. With high heat, students have a harder time concentrating, and cognitive function can be impaired.[40] Schools, especially those without sufficient air conditioning, become intolerable and this affects learning and teaching. Black and Latino students, who are exposed to more hot days, perform worse on standardized tests. In fact, heat and uncomfortable classrooms in one study accounted for 5 percent of the gap in performance between Black and white students.[41] The 2023 EPA report on children and climate change noted that this lost learning will decrease potential future income for *each* graduating cohort by an estimated $6.9 billion.[42]

Students' exposure to high heat will increase as climate change worsens. Heat islands are areas that are on average 1.25°F hotter than the surrounding community. Climate change is increasing the number of communities experiencing heat island effects and the number of students who attend school in heat islands. The Trust for Public Land estimated that, in 2019, more than one-third of the 50 million students enrolled in public schools attended schools in a heat island.[43] Of those students, over 4 million were in areas of "severe" heat islands (7°F above the surrounding community temperature) and over 1 million were in an extreme heat island (10°F or more above the surrounding community temperature). That last number of students in extreme heat islands had increased by 32 percent since 2013. Low-income students disproportionately attend schools in these heat islands partly because of limited green space and tree cover in the surrounding community. Extreme heat is already a barrier to educators' efforts to advance equity, and it's getting hotter.

Disproportionate Impact

Climate change will affect everyone, but it will not affect everyone equally. Black, Indigenous, Latino, and other communities of color as well as low-income rural and urban communities are disproportionately affected negatively from climate change. Long-lasting discriminatory housing policies have left many low-income urban communities of color in areas more prone to flooding.[44] Fewer trees leave these communities more vulnerable to heat island effects.[45] Policy decisions, including placements of highways, also mean these communities experience worse air pollution and as a result suffer from health consequences like asthma at higher rates.[46] Alaskan Native communities face increased food insecurity because climate change is devastating many traditional food sources that are critical to their nutrition and culture.[47] Under-resourced rural communities are also more vulnerable to the impacts of climate change and have less access to capital to help them rebuild.[48] A 2022 US Government Accountability Office (GAO) report found that schools in socially vulnerable communities experienced more challenges responding to extreme weather. They had a harder time providing the emotional and academic supports needed to help students recover as well as accessing the financial and instructional resources to rebuild.[49]

These are just some examples of the unequal impact of climate change here in the United States. While this book is focused on issues domestically, it is essential to acknowledge the unequal impact of climate change at a global scale. The Global South, in particular, bears the brunt of climate impacts due to economic, health, and infrastructure inequities as well as geographic susceptibility.[50] In August 2021, UNICEF released a report identifying climate change as a child rights crisis and introducing the Children's Climate Risk Index, which looked at exposure to climate and environmental hazards (water scarcity, heat, etc.) alongside child vulnerability (poverty, access to education).[51] The report found that nearly every child on Earth is at risk from negative impacts related to climate change, and 1 billion (nearly half of all children on the planet) live in countries facing extremely high risk and are exposed to multiple overlapping hazards.

THERE'S HOPE BECAUSE WE CAN ADVANCE SOLUTIONS

In 2018, one student felt depressed under the unbearable weight of understanding the climate impacts. Looking for a way to channel this fear, she learned from other student movements, notably the March for Our Lives movement in response to the Parkland school shooting, and made the decision to strike from school. On her flyers, she wrote, "My name is Greta, I am in ninth grade, and I am school-striking for the climate. Since you adults don't give a damn about my future, I won't either."[52]

During her first strike, Greta Thunberg sat alone with a sign. Just over a year later, at the age of sixteen, she was named TIME *Person of the Year. The* TIME *article noted: "Thunberg has no magic solution. But she has succeeded in creating a global attitudinal shift, transforming millions of vague, middle-of-the-night anxieties into a worldwide movement calling for urgent change."*[53]

There is no one magical solution to climate change, but there are solutions we can and need to advance. As leaders in education, we can show young people we do care about their future, and we can help them understand what they can do. We can show them that they don't have to strike from school to feel like they are making a difference.

Considering the main drivers and the impacts of climate change, climate solutions generally focus on two related areas of work: climate mitigation and climate adaptation. Given the need for all sectors, industries, communities, and governments to engage in climate solutions and the critical opportunity to advance equity as we advance solutions, our framework for schools includes four key questions:

1. *Climate mitigation*: What are the main drivers of our greenhouse gas pollution, and how can we reduce our pollution to mitigate our contribution to climate change?
2. *Climate adaptation*: How does climate change impact our schools, and what can we do to adapt and build resilience?
3. *Unique role of education*: What is the unique role of education and our schools in helping to advance climate solutions?
4. *Equity*: How does climate change differentially impact the students, communities, and schools we serve, and how, in taking action on climate, can we advance equity?

What Is Climate Mitigation?

To advance solutions related to climate mitigation, we must address two key questions: What are the main drivers of carbon pollution for schools, and how can we reduce those emissions to decrease our impact on climate change?

Let's consider our two biggest drivers of emissions in the United States: transportation and electricity. Examples of mitigation solutions include transitioning vehicles from gas-powered to electric and shifting our electricity grid to renewable or clean energy sources like solar power, wind, or nuclear energy. It's true that these solutions come with different trade-offs. For instance, batteries for electric vehicles rely on critical minerals that need to be mined. While trade-offs should be considered and addressed, we know the extensive damage our reliance on fossil fuels has caused for us, our climate, and our environment. We cannot allow this damage to continue, and we must consider a range of solutions to reduce our reliance on fossil fuels dramatically.

Efforts to accelerate mitigation solutions can't be considered only on a national level. Individuals, local communities, and schools all play a critical role in advancing mitigation solutions within their own context. In chapter 5, we go into more detail about the range of opportunities to support schools in getting to net-zero emissions. To accomplish this, schools should consider the overlap of their needs with some of our biggest emitting sectors. Carbon pollution from schools comes from the combustion of fossil fuels, whether on-site in our heating, ventilation, and air-conditioning (HVAC) systems and in our transportation systems (diesel school buses, school-owned cars) or offsite in the production of our food; in the manufacturing of the materials used to construct and operate schools; or in the generation of the electricity used to power computers, lights, and other electric machines. To advance solutions related to electricity, schools can consider generating renewable energy either on-site or using renewable energy through utility agreements. For buildings, schools can shift from fossil-fuel-burning furnaces and boilers to electricity-powered heat pumps to provide heat and cooling. For transportation, schools can shift from diesel to electric buses.

These solutions may seem daunting and expensive; however, adopting a "getting to zero" mind-set and bringing that mind-set to every decision and opportunity can get schools there over time.[54] Central to getting to zero over time is having a strategic plan and leveraging opportunities as they present themselves. For instance, if a new school building is being constructed, can it be built to be net-zero and generate as much electricity as it consumes? If an HVAC system breaks down, are there policies to replace legacy technology that burn fossil fuels with new modern technology that runs on clean energy?[55] Although not every school or community is the same, there are similar significant drivers of emissions, and schools can do a lot and learn from emerging models to fulfill their responsibility to reduce environmental impacts.

What Is Climate Adaptation?

To advance solutions related to climate adaptation, we must consider the likely climate risks and impacts for schools, and what we can do to adapt and build resilience. Climate adaptation recognizes the consequences of living in a changing climate and seeks to reduce vulnerability to the impacts. Scientists have confirmed that we will be living with the impacts of climate change for some time, so all of society—including our schools—needs to consider adaptation solutions in conjunction with mitigation solutions. In some circumstances, these solutions can prove beneficial to both efforts.

Mitigation solutions largely depend on emissions reduction; adaptation solutions depend on climate risk and vulnerability. Climate risk and vulnerability often vary based on local or regional geography. For instance, the western United States is more susceptible to drought, heat, wildfires, and flooding from atmospheric rivers. The Gulf Coast experiences climate risks with sea level rise, more intense hurricanes, and heat. Flooding, often the costliest climate consequence, will impact communities across the country. Regional adaptation efforts may include strategies to build better early warning systems for extreme weather, planting mangrove forests to reduce storm surge, raising streets to prevent flooding, and creating cooling centers to reduce exposure to high heat. In each case, adaptation strategies depend on the local context.

There are adaptation strategies that schools and school districts can apply as well. In chapter 4, we go into more detail about the range of opportunities available to schools to address climate impacts and advance adaptation solutions. A critical aspect to this will require forward thinking, which we are not often accustomed to doing. It will require us to consider our probable futures and how we might adapt.[56] Schools need to absorb what these impacts might mean for them in 2030, 2035, and beyond. For instance, for a school in a community where the days over 90°F are projected to increase significantly, is there opportunity to ensure sufficient cooling and transition heat-trapping asphalt schoolyards to sustainable green spaces with sufficient shade? In an area susceptible to extreme storms or wildfires, do schools have sufficient mental health supports for students to process climate-related anxiety and cope with trauma in the wake of destructive extreme weather? Schools can develop plans to continue learning and student supports in preparation for climate-related closures. And schools in every community can consider their broader role as hubs of resilience for the community. For instance, schools equipped with solar and battery storage can shelter community members in the event of power outages, creating a space where people can plug in and access emergency services and cooling. Adaptation solutions push us to hold future mind-sets that assume instability and changes from our previous life experiences.

What Is the Unique Role for K–12 Schools?

To build a more sustainable world, we must consider the education sector's own unique value-added contributions to climate solutions. As we mentioned in chapter 1, education is key to all solutions. With 50 million students enrolled annually in the United States, schools are uniquely positioned to engage students in learning about climate change, possible solutions, and sustainability to help prepare them to live and succeed in a changing climate.

Climate change is a dynamic issue and there are many opportunities to unlock this learning. We see the following components as a basis for climate learning. Schools should help students understand climate science—starting with the greenhouse gas effect and how it is impacting our climate and weather systems. Schools should help students understand how climate change impacts our society, economy, policies, and health. Schools should engage students in learning about climate solutions, including renewable energy, coastal restoration, and composting. They should expose students to different career pathways, including renewable energy, sustainable engineering, and wildfire control. They can help students process climate change through the arts, music, and literature and help students understand how they can activate policy change through civics. And they should help build students' understanding that we depend on our environment to thrive.

Learning is essential for the societal transformation we need. In unlocking the power of education, people across our society will better understand our changing world and what we all can do to advance solutions. It will catalyze long-lasting change for generations to come.

How Does Climate Change Impact Equity?

To advance a more just and equitable society as we advance climate solutions, we must consider how climate change differentially impacts the populations we serve and how, in taking action on climate, we can advance equity. The patterns of inequity in our educational structures and our environmental reality overlap, and they do not exist in isolation. Black, Latino, Indigenous, and other students of color, as well as students from under-resourced urban and rural communities, disproportionately experience education inequality and environmental injustice. The fundamental societal shift needed to address climate change presents an opportunity to right these injustices and advance a more equitable society.

As education leaders consider advancing solutions, they have an opportunity to start by bringing students and parents from these communities to the table. In polling, Black (81 percent) and Latino (83 percent) respondents have indicated higher levels of concern about climate change than white respondents (70 percent).[57] Indigenous communities have consistently led the efforts to address climate change and advocate to protect the Earth. Engaging students and families from these communities can help ensure meaningful solutions that advance equity, reflect community needs and their level of concern, and leverage community assets and leadership.

In addition to engaging communities, existing inequities must be acknowledged and addressed. For instance, under-resourced schools have less access to capital to make investments in sustainable infrastructure, but focused attention on these schools and increasing opportunities for investments to decarbonize them can have downstream benefits too, for example, improved health and decreased operations costs. Ensuring that students from under-resourced communities have the opportunity to build the knowledge and skills necessary for success in the new economy can help improve economic mobility.

If we do not focus on equity while advancing climate solutions, we may further exacerbate existing patterns of an unjust society. If we consider how inequity cuts across our society, including education, health, economy, and environment, we can advance solutions that make progress toward a more just world.

Key Takeaways

1. *It's warming*: Our atmosphere acts as a heat-trapping blanket, which historically has created conditions on Earth for life to thrive. By emitting carbon pollution, we are changing the material of the atmosphere, trapping more heat and warming our planet.
2. *It's us*: Our carbon pollution, primarily associated with the burning of fossil fuels, related to electricity, transportation, buildings, manufacturing, and food is driving climate change. It is further accelerated by removal of carbon sinks, including forests, mangroves, and other naturally occurring sinks.
3. *It's impacting us now*: Climate change is already and will increasingly impact student health, well-being, learning, and opportunity. While all students experience these impacts, they are worse for Black, Latino, Indigenous, and other students of color as well as students from under-resourced rural and urban communities.
4. *There are solutions we can advance today*: Schools can play a pivotal role in advancing solutions to reduce carbon pollution, adapt and build resilience, educate and empower students, and advance equity to ensure a just transition.

3

Supporting Teaching and Learning to Prepare Students to Lead a Sustainable Future

***IN JUNE 2020,** New Jersey became the first state in the United States to adopt cross-curricular climate change standards. The move made headlines for both the ambition and the recognition that climate change is not merely a subject to be explored in science but one that can be understood through the arts, health, social studies, world languages, and more.*

First Lady of New Jersey Tammy Snyder Murphy led the effort to enact the cross-curricular climate change standards. She recognized not only the threats from climate change but also the urgency and necessity to help young people process the world they live in and what they can do. She stated:

> Our collective mission—resolving the damage that human activity has done to the environment since the 19th century—is an incredible burden that our children and grandchildren will have to face. But, the adoption of these standards is much more than an added educational

requirement, it is a symbol of a partnership between generations. And, together we will begin to undo the damage we have caused.[1]

In New Jersey, state curriculum standards undergo a review process by a committee every five years. The committee is composed of more than 130 educators across the state. In 2019, Murphy raised the idea of climate change standards in the group's opening meeting. She remained persistent throughout the work of the committee and subcommittees and, as she described, was "impressed, inspired, and encouraged" watching the educators make these standards real.[2]

To prepare to implement the standards, New Jersey partnered with nonprofit SubjectToClimate to create a hub of resources for educators, including lesson plans, professional learning, and more. In 2023, New Jersey established an office of climate education within its state department of education.[3] *As the state continues implementation, Murphy sees this work as central to the future well-being of the state. Whether it's preparing students for jobs in a clean economy or creating innovations to help New Jersey adapt to the impacts it faces, education is essential to the state's climate efforts. Murphy recognized that "this generation of students is inspired and determined to fix the climate crisis. Ask any teacher and he or she will tell you—a motivated student can achieve anything."*[4]

Engaging students in learning; helping students develop, explore, and think; and fostering understanding is core to the work of all educators. As it relates to climate change, however, this core is lacking today. Four years after their adoption, New Jersey remains the only state with cross-curricular climate change standards. As of 2020, twenty-nine states and Washington, DC, included human-caused climate change in their science standards, and five states required it in social studies classes.[5] While the presence or absence of climate change in state standards can signal whether students have the opportunity to learn about it, it does not guarantee it. Standards define what students should know and be able to do, but curricula—lessons and materials—often determine what is taught in the classroom.

There is a lot of work to be done to ensure young people understand the changing world they are facing, but leaders across the country, like Murphy, are taking steps to make that happen. In this chapter, we highlight the state of education on climate change across the country; key questions to guide thinking on climate education; and the stories of educators, school leaders, and administrators utilizing climate education mind-sets to help children build knowledge and skills necessary for success in a changing climate. There are many opportunities to integrate climate in learning beyond what we outline below. With these stories, we hope to elevate how these mind-sets can help administrators, school leaders, and educators find partnerships, build consensus, and create system-level approaches to climate education.

VARIABILITY IN CLIMATE LEARNING

In a 2022 survey on people's opinions about climate change, 82 percent of respondents agreed with the following statement: "Children will be essential in fighting climate change and we must give them the knowledge and skills to build a sustainable world."[6] The respondents ran the spectrum from extremely worried about climate change to least worried about climate change, and yet there was broad agreement to support education, a consistent finding from a broad range of surveys on the topic.

The North American Association of Environmental Education (NAAEE) commissioned a national survey on the state of climate education and found 74 percent of educators and 80 percent of administrators think it is our responsibility to teach students about climate change in school.[7] The survey also suggested that educators and administrators worry about parents' pushback and politics on the issue. Yet educators' fear of complaints may not always be an accurate reflection of community beliefs. That is, educators' perceptions of resistance to climate education may be overstated, or it may come from a small but loud portion of a community.

The Yale Program on Climate Change Communication (YPCCC) has studied public opinion on climate change for years and uses an analysis to group public opinion into "Six Americas": The Alarmed, Concerned, Cautious, Disengaged, Doubtful, and Dismissive. As of fall 2023, 56 percent of all Americans fell into the "alarmed" or "concerned" category combined, while 23 percent fell in the "doubtful" or "dismissive" category combined.[8] In other words, people who are concerned about climate represent more than double the number of people dismissive of the issue. And this concern has been increasing as the impacts of climate change are growing more present in our lives. The work of the YPCCC consistently finds that teaching students about global warming in schools polls among the most popular solutions to advance on climate change, with 75 percent of their respondents in agreement. In a presentation, the founder and director of the YPCCC, Dr. Anthony Leiserowitz, remarked, "In every single county in America you have a substantial majority of Americans who support climate being taught by our schools. That's true in Texas, it's true in Oklahoma, it's true in Wyoming, and North Dakota and West Virginia and Alaska; all of our big, large fossil fuel patches. People everywhere think this is an important thing that we should be doing for our kids."[9]

Despite the broad consensus, climate change is not taught sufficiently in America's schools, thus preventing today's students from learning critical concepts about the world they stand to inherit. The variability across learning experiences for students can be significant. In her book *Miseducation: How Climate Change Is Taught in America*, Katie Worth traveled to different states to understand this issue better.[10] In reflecting on her experience, she noted that there are "intrepid teachers in every district in America, probably who care about this issue, who think that kids deserve to know about the world that they're entering, and who give kids in their classes a really great education about it. But there's also often a teacher in the very next room that is giving them misinformation or totally ignoring the subject, even if it is in the standards."[11]

In a report from the National Center for Science Education (NCSE), Oklahoma received a B– for its coverage of climate change in state science standards.[12] The science standards include climate change, and they have some alignment with the Next Generation Science Standards (NGSS). However, they delete critical components of the language from NGSS related to climate change that are essential to build student understanding of the causes of climate change.

In 2017, Melissa Lau, a middle school teacher in Oklahoma, developed an interest in place-based experiences to further her understanding of science.[13] She first engaged in a project with the University of Oklahoma where she spent a week on a tributary studying how freshwater mussels were impacted by pollution from nearby commercial farms. The next year, Melissa spent about a month in Alaska with the PolarTREC program, which connects educators and researchers, and where she studied vegetation change in the warming Arctic.[14] She indicated these experiences "pushed the urgency" for her on climate change. She understood that "what we are doing is not enough. The urgency isn't being brought to our students." She then began to teach climate change more explicitly in her classroom. Knowing her community—and knowing that Oklahomans have a deep connection to the land—Melissa grounded her teaching in the impacts in Oklahoma and its ecosystems. Although she was nervous that she would be met with resistance, she was surprised by the amount of support rather than pushback that she received. Her work fell in line with the state standards, and she received full support from her school administration. While some challenges came from stakeholders outside her school, in her school and her classroom, she found little opposition. The NCSE helped her to identify resources with misinformation on climate change. While teaching, Melissa helped students understand how to think critically about any misinformation being presented. To sort through the noise, Melissa recognized all people in the system need a better understanding of climate change in order to build collaboration across educators, administrators, and school board members.

Today, that collaboration is lacking in many schools, districts, and states across the country. In the NAAEE survey, only 21 percent of educators felt "very informed" about climate change, and only 14 percent felt "very prepared" to teach about it.[15] By comparison, educators in Brazil, Canada, France, and India are three times as likely to say they have the support to teach about climate change and sustainability compared to educators in the United States.[16] In the United States, educators identify time, curriculum, resources, preparedness, and understanding as barriers to teaching climate change in school.[17] Organizations like SubjectToClimate are trying to change that by curating a searchable database of climate lesson plans aligned with state standards, professional learning opportunities for educators, and resources related to climate content. Collaborative efforts like the one between the University of California, California State University, and the nonprofit Ten Strands, called the Environmental and Climate Change Literacy Projects (ECCLPs), seek to provide preservice support for educators in California teacher preparation programs.[18]

Given the variability in learning experiences as well as the barriers that teachers face, it's not surprising that students have misconceptions, worry, and seek alternate sources for information. A survey from *Education Week* revealed the depth of students' misconceptions about the climate and found that over half of the respondents turned to social media to learn more about climate change, which runs the risks of further exposure to inaccurate or false information.[19]

Our schools need to help empower a climate literate generation—a generation with the understanding, knowledge, and skills necessary to succeed in a changing climate. As a base, a foundational understanding of climate change is critical. With This Is Planet Ed in partnership with The Nature Conservancy and their lead climate scientists, we worked to modify the essential climate understandings from YPCCC described in chapter 2 and break them down for children and youth. We outlined four essential climate principles that children and youth should understand.[20]

1. *Earth is our home*: Our Earth has an invisible blanket of heat-trapping gases that traps just the right amount of heat to keep our Earth the perfect temperature for us to live—it's not too hot and it's not too cold. This helps students understand that we depend on our Earth to live, giving them a base-level understanding of our climate system.
2. *It's getting hotter because of us*: A thin sheet is different from a heavy blanket, and how thick our blanket is matters. Right now, we humans are adding more heat-trapping gases to the atmosphere, making the "blanket" thicker. This extra carbon pollution comes from electricity (how we power on), transportation (how we get around), manufacturing (how we make things), food (how we grow things to eat), buildings (how we live), and land use (how we change the land and take care of nature). All the carbon pollution is building up in the atmosphere, and it's making the planet hotter. This helps students understand the current change in our climate system as well as the causes—how humans are making the planet hotter. To advance solutions with the most meaningful impact, students need to understand what is causing the problem.
3. *It's changing now, and it's impacting us*: A hotter planet changes our climate. Wet is wetter, dry is drier, and hot is hotter. Storms, floods, and wildfires are more dangerous. This is changing what we do, the way we work, and how we live. It's impacting us all, but it is hurting some people more than others: people who have less are being hurt more, and that's not fair. This helps students understand the consequences—the change is here now, how it impacts us, and how people are impacted differently.
4. *But together, we can make the changes we need for a brighter future*: We can stop polluting our atmosphere and help our communities stay safe. We can make a difference—in our homes, our schools, and our communities—when we work together. We can create a pathway to a brighter future. This principle is critical. It empowers students to understand that there are things that we can all do to make a difference.

In addition to these essential principles, educators must recognize that climate is a cross-cutting issue that has an impact on all facets of our society. When they recognize the transdisciplinary nature of climate change at a deeper level, educators can find ways to apply climate change as a lens for their teaching across subjects to develop climate knowledge. In science, students can build understandings of the greenhouse gas effect, ocean acidification, and renewable energy. In social studies, students can learn about how climate impacts the economy, how to build a resilient community, or how government can be used as a lever for change. In health, students can learn strategies to keep themselves and others healthy in a changing climate. In English, art, and music, students can engage in creative ways to process their feelings or communicate the issue to others. And in career and technical education, students can learn about climate-specific jobs or how to apply a sustainability lens to any job. Acknowledging our changing climate can be a scary thing to process, and students are facing increased eco-anxiety. Schoolwide support for social emotional learning, developmentally appropriate learning, and strong adult-student relationships are critical.

On February 7, 2022, the Los Angeles City Board of Education passed a resolution to increase climate literacy throughout the district. With the resolution, the district specifically committed "to transforming our teaching of climate change to meet the scale and urgency of the crises by implementing, infusing, and developing climate change education across all curricula, and in every grade PK–12, a commitment that will require the allocation of significant resources."[21] The resolution established a climate literacy task force to coordinate action, infuse climate-related learning opportunities across curricula, and support educators—work that all districts should follow.

Preparing the rising generation for success in a changing climate requires us to empower them with the understanding, knowledge, and skills to advance a sustainable world. To prepare the next generation for success, school leaders, administrators, and educators need to think critically about ways to integrate climate perspectives across the curriculum, ensure that educators feel prepared and confident to teach about climate change, and support students so they feel empowered to take action. To shift mind-sets toward education on climate change, school leaders should consider the following questions.

Climate Education Questions

- How are we helping children understand our relationship to our climate and environment from an early age? How do we support students in building a foundational understanding of our changing climate?
- How should we apply a climate lens across grades and subjects to enable students to develop climate knowledge to understand holistically the causes, consequences, and solutions to climate change and prepare students for jobs in a clean economy?
- How are we providing social emotional support to help students process complex and challenging climate topics?
- How should informal learning and extracurricular opportunities provide deeper engagement for students on climate education? How should we collaborate with partners across the community to further enhance climate-related learning opportunities for students?
- How should we ensure educators feel prepared and supported to teach climate across the curriculum?

Climate Education Mind-Set

To have a climate education mind-set, school leaders, administrators, and educators should:

- Understand the essential climate principles and that we depend on our climate and environment to thrive.
- Seek opportunities to integrate learning about climate throughout existing lessons, curricula, and activities and ensure that teaching about climate change is connected to solutions.

- Create space for social emotional learning and strong adult-student relationships to foster a safe learning environment for students to grapple with complex problems.
- Partner with other educators and the broader community to engage students in deeper cross-disciplinary learning on climate change, including exposing students to clean economy career pathways.
- Ensure that educators and the school community feel confident, prepared, and supported in engaging students in learning about climate change—its causes, consequences, and solutions.

In education, it is our responsibility to help students make sense of the world, prepare them for jobs, enable them to become engaged citizens, and help them achieve their potential. I (Laura) recently heard a remark that stories of the present day that fail to incorporate the context of climate change are works of science fiction. If we educate students today without taking into account climate change, we are preparing them for a world that is science fiction—for a world that will not exist or be recognizable as we know it today. This is educational malpractice. It prevents students from achieving their potential. We must do all that we can to set students up for success. We must help them process, understand, and prepare to live and succeed in a changing climate.

PREPARING STUDENTS FOR SUCCESS BY CONNECTING TO LOCAL CONTEXT AND ENVIRONMENT

> It's important that we all recognize that human beings are dependent upon the natural world.
>
> —Megan Bang, professor of learning sciences, Northwestern University

Universal Design for Learning (UDL) offers a framework to help remove barriers from teaching and learning and maximize success for diverse learners. Based in the science of learning and recognizing the variability that exists across learners, UDL pushes educators to provide students with multiple means of engagement. Engagement is essential for effective student learning: an engaged learner builds understanding, whereas disengagement is a barrier to understanding.[22] A UDL guideline to support educators in providing multiple means of engagement is "to optimize relevance, value, and authenticity" for learning.

When they think about climate change, many people visualize a polar bear on a melting ice sheet. While this may appeal to young people who may be interested in learning about animals, focusing on polar bears distances the issue from students' actual experience. Most children have never seen a polar bear in real life (and won't), and a changing climate far away in the Arctic may be hard to grasp. It is not directly relevant to the lives of most students. By connecting climate education to local communities and environments, we can make the issue more relevant for students.

Indigenous communities have effectively integrated connections across environment, culture, language, and disciplines for generations. The deep relationships with the environment, including the land, water, and natural resources, are central to Indigenous cultures. The relationship with the environment is woven into traditional language and food. Since time immemorial, these relationships have been developed and passed on through each generation. Indigenous Knowledge Systems (IKS) consider the deep, interwoven connections that shape the relationship between humans and the environment. In a piece on how education can advance action on climate change, Owen Oliver of the Quinault Indian Nation reflected, "Schools can partner with tribes to create curricula that are based on the original caretakers' stories and strides. Because if we are able to connect students to the teachings of the land and the importance of all people's stories to the land, we will be able to gain a collective push to protect what has given us life: The Earth."[23]

The impacts of climate change are different based on geography: flooding in Kentucky, droughts in the Southwest, sea-level rise in Massachusetts and Florida. When educators consider and draw connections for students about how climate impacts them, their community, and the environment locally, students better understand how such issues have immediate relevance in their lives. For instance, New Harmony High School in New Orleans, Louisiana, supports students in "fostering an interconnectedness of people, land, air, and water that prepares students for college, careers, and beyond."[24] Their mission is to "educate diverse problem solvers rooted in their communities and informed by a greater social and environmental context."[25] One of the ways they fulfill this mission is by having students engage directly in coastal restoration projects to support adaptation for the broader New Orleans community. With this focus, they help students build understanding about how climate change impacts their community and how to advance locally based solutions. In Hawai'i, the Pacific American Foundation (PAF)—grounded in the understanding of *ma ka hana ka 'ike* ("through doing one learns")—works with students to restore a fishpond, thus connecting students to their land and their culture.[26] As these examples demonstrate, educators have many opportunities to engage students in hands-on learning and connect them to their environment and solutions.

Education about climate change can happen in a variety of settings: in classrooms; in museums; through media and out-of-school education; and the outdoors, a critically important setting for engaging students. Climate change education creates opportunities for teaching and learning about the relationship between human activity; local communities; and the environments we live, work, and play in. All students need the opportunity to learn that we depend on our environment to thrive and that our decisions and actions can impact the environment for the good or bad.

As the UDL framework outlines, the affective networks of the brain drive the why of learning.[27] Teaching about climate change, connected to that local context, can motivate students to understand why. It creates opportunities to connect to their lived experience; opportunities for students to grapple with real-world problems; and, most important, opportunities for students to generate meaningful solutions.

Learning in Places: Seattle Public Schools

Dr. Megan Bang served as a commissioner with K12 Climate Action. Megan is of Ojibwe and Italian descent, and she is a professor of learning sciences at Northwestern University, where she has a deep commitment to improving science learning environments for children to help them develop more meaningful understandings across culture, families, communities, and the natural world. In an interview for *Harvard EdCast*, Megan remarked, "I come to this work as a native woman, I think about human relationships to the natural world as fundamental to who we are."[28] For several years, Megan has worked in partnership with Dr. Carrie Tzou, a professor of education at University of Washington Bothell, and Seattle Public Schools to develop and engage students in holistic science learning through an initiative called Learning in Places.[29]

Learning in Places is a "collaborative network of educators, families, and community partners working to cultivate equitable, culturally thriving, socio-ecological systems learning and ethical decision-making using field-based science education in outdoor places, including gardens, for children in pre-kindergarten to 5th grade (and beyond) and their families." The goal of Learning in Places is to leverage science education as a vehicle to help shape "just, sustainable, and culturally thriving communities."[30] To do this, they focus on four key concepts: nature cultural relationships, collective well-being, ethical reasoning, and routinely getting outside to learn in nature.

Carrie presented before the K12 Climate Action Commission showing two powerful visuals to highlight models we hold about human relationships with the environment.[31] In the first visual, a human is represented on the top of a pyramid with animals and the natural world below. This represents the notion of nature cultural divides, in other words, that we, as humans, are separate and dominant and that we can control and manipulate the natural world. This visual represents the assumptions that too many hold in our society—we, humans, are dominant. A second visual showed a circle with humans represented alongside animals and the natural world to represent nature cultural relations. Humans are, in fact, part of the natural world, and the relationship is one of interdependency. This second visual represents the model we need to restore our relationship with the natural world.

In addition to fostering this concept of nature cultural relations, Learning in Places focused on co-design. Co-design includes family engagement, routinely getting kids in the natural environment, and engaging them in understanding ethical dimensions of science. The initiative sought to leverage "porous" learning opportunities, recognizing that learning from family and culture bleed into learning in school. As an example, they focused on engaging students in conversations about the seasons. Megan noted, "We did that because one of the things that's happening with changing climates is that seasonal patterns are shifting. And many of our families pointed out that a lot of their cultural practices revolved around seasons. . . . It was a way for us to build a model that deeply connected culture and identity and everyday routine practices with some of the deep sciences that are connected to changing climates."[32] In connecting closely with families and building these porous learning opportunities, they emphasize the importance of collective well-being: that we depend on each other to thrive.

To understand ethical decision making further, Learning in Places asked students to consider "should we" questions. Science typically focuses on "can we" questions, which reinforces the notion of nature cultural divides, but "should we" questions require deeper-level thinking about the consequences of our actions. As the impacts of a changing climate accelerate, "should we" questions are becoming increasingly essential for us all to consider, whether you are a scientist, a business leader, a policy maker, a teacher, a student, or a family. For instance, should we continue to allow new development in a fire-prone area, should we expand a pipeline, should we continue to sell a fossil-fuel-dependent product, or should we take public transportation or drive? Reframing these questions and helping support learners at an early age in asking these questions can help develop the critical thinkers and problem solvers society needs.

Critically important to this work is routinely getting children outside to learn in the natural world. Even with as little as fifteen minutes, students across all settings—rural, suburban, and urban—can get outside and interact and observe nature. This routine practice fosters more meaningful connections and curiosity about our relationship with the natural world.

Prompted by these questions, deeper learning enables students to develop skills that include critical thinking, collaboration, and communication.[33] Curricula and pedagogy like Learning in Places that take student-centered or inquiry-based approaches enable students to learn about relevant real-world problems and brainstorm solutions. Education leaders can partner with researchers, families, and communities to consider effective ways not only to teach the facts of climate change but also to consider more deeply how to engage students in developing the knowledge, skills, understandings, and ways of thinking needed to build a more sustainable future.

PREPARING STUDENTS FOR SUCCESS IN THE CLEAN ECONOMY

> Finding shared common interests . . . it's something our world desperately needs right now, and, for climate change, that has to happen. It's making those relationships happen, outside of getting into the politics of it. Because we all [want] the best for our generations ahead.
>
> —Tammie Delaney, former school board member, Hayden School District

As our economy makes the necessary shift away from fossil fuels, new jobs are being created. Investments from the Inflation Reduction Act are projected to create 9 million jobs in the next decade.[34] Some of these jobs will be in the expansion of renewable energy industries, like solar and wind. Other existing professions may require more people than currently employed today. For instance, with the push to electrify everything, we need a lot more electricians. In an interview, the environmentalist Bill McKibben remarked, "If you know a young person who wants to do something that's going to help the world and wants to make a good living at the same time, tell them to go become an electrician."[35]

In addition to these more specific jobs, all professions—whether fashion designer, chef, business leader, doctor, farmer, policy maker, or educator—will need to work within a changing climate. People within these professions will need knowledge to do their job effectively in a changing climate. This type of career development is similar to the shift we saw when computers and related technology became ubiquitous. We now have specialized professions in fields like information technology, but most other professionals also require base-level proficiency with technology.

Schools need to ensure that students are ready for these shifts, and career and technical education (CTE) can provide an opportunity to help prepare students for success in the clean economy. CTE programs expose students to different career paths and provide hands-on training and work-based learning. CTE clusters generally focus on different pathways, including agriculture, food, and natural resources; manufacturing; architecture and construction; and more.[36] Expanding programs to fill the demand for specific clean energy jobs and adapting all programs to incorporate sustainability are essential.

Hayden School District

In the early 1900s, the historic Hayden Granary in Hayden, Colorado, was filled with seed and was used as a central meeting point for Hayden-area farmers and ranchers. Today, the granary, previously slated to be torn down, has been revitalized with a bustling coffee shop, brewery, wine bar, and more—all thanks to Tammie and Patrick Delaney.[37] "Every community has that social hub," noted Tammie. When the Delaneys first opened Wild Goose Coffee at the granary, Tammie recalled, "We saw people who, if they were on social media, they would probably never talk to each other, suddenly connecting and finding shared common interest." The commitment to community and finding common ground and connection is central to Tammie's perspective, both as a small business owner and a former Hayden School District school board president and board member.

Located in the northwest part of Colorado, the Hayden School District serves about 435 students from preschool through twelfth grade in one complex. According to the strategic plan for the district, a Hayden learner is equipped and courageous, a critical thinker, globally aware and civically engaged, and independent and confident. In particular, the plan notes, "Hayden students apply global perspectives to take action in their local context."[38]

The local economy of Hayden and Yampa Valley was traditionally based on agriculture and ranching, and also on their proximity to the popular ski town Steamboat and, for decades, coal. These pillars of Hayden's economy are being impacted by climate change and the transition to clean energy. Extreme weather and heat threaten farming production and the ski season. For economic reasons and to reduce carbon pollution, the coal-fired power plant is slated for closure.[39]

Recognizing this uncertain economic future and the need for more sustainably focused work opportunities for students, Tammie was a key leader on the school board to help expand career pathways for students and to engage Hayden in what is now called the Yampa Valley Partnership for Students, Stewardship, and Sustainability (YVPS3).[40] This hub is a partnership between four K–12 school districts, two institutions of higher education, and several industry partners. It was created with support from the nonprofit Lyra Colorado, which seeks to connect rural school districts with each other and community colleges to drive "education, climate resilience, and economic prosperity."[41] In 2021, a Hayden and South Routt school district partnership received a $1 million grant from the state of Colorado to further develop curriculum and engage students in understanding sustainable agriculture, energy, and local food systems. These programs engage students in work-based learning opportunities with local producers, including farmers focused on regenerative agriculture. Achieving this success, though, required community buy-in.

Tammie and other community leaders focused efforts on building collaboration and stewardship. She noted, "One of the things we all have in common: we want clean air, clean water, [and] great soil to grow and produce food." Well before she was on the school board, Tammie was committed to stewardship. She described it as "something that I've been working on for arguably, my lifetime." Tammie recognized that connecting students to sustainable agriculture can help build a more sustainable world. She noted, "Kids that have that opportunity and have been raised on farms and ranches are very close to the land, and so the premise of that work ethic and sense of purpose, sense of responsibility, sense of something beyond themselves is like a gift." Developing these perspectives and skills, she added, "can translate into any job."

In bringing this issue up with the broader community in Hayden, Tammie and the team understood the need to focus on common interests. The district conducted surveys to better understand what students wanted, and they found significant interest in expanding educational opportunities in agriculture. Student demand can be one catalyst for action. The other catalyst Tammie identified was a common, unifying language. She knew that leading with the word "climate" would have further polarized a discussion that needs to be interest-based rather than positionally based to understand the need and opportunity at hand. This was especially true because three of the four districts in the rural collaborative are very affected by the transition away from coal, having depended on coal for decades. By using the words "stewardship and sustainability," Tammie and her partners emphasized the community's common values: "This is about building soil. This is about water. This is about how to ensure that the generations to come have an environment that not only people, but livestock, plants, and produce can thrive. No one can argue about that."

Although the district collaborative has had initial success with the work, Tammie anticipates potential challenges ahead. Transitions in school district leadership can hamper the initiative's longevity, especially when collaborating across four school districts. Tammie knows that this makes the need for teamwork even more critical. Focusing on broader partnerships, building and maintaining relationships with local producers, and fostering buy-in from the community helps the school district weather any changes in leadership.

Tammie has advice for others embarking on efforts in their own community. She emphasizes the need to "focus on the process, not necessarily the outcome." Relationships and building buy-in is a long-term effort. She noted, "Putting several leaders in the room together that had not worked much together—[it] took time to get to know each other and understand common interests." But ultimately for the Hayden community, that investment in building relationships paid off because it enabled them to create opportunities for students to learn more deeply about local climate-related issues, sustainability, and career pathways to foster a rising generation of environmental stewards.

CONCLUSION

People will be the driving force behind the local, national, and global solutions we need to address our changing climate now and in the decades to come. Climate change affects every part of our society, from business to education, agriculture to health care. Recognizing that our world now exists in a changing climate and ensuring students are prepared to live and succeed in that changing climate are fundamental to the work of educators. An understanding of our connection to our environment, climate change, and sustainability is essential for all people, and our schools must do their part to help our society develop climate literacy. Researchers have identified education as underutilized but necessary for society to address climate change, and we've only just scratched the surface of its potential.[42]

Schools and afterschool programs across the country are currently helping students understand what they need to know to live well in a changing climate, but there is so much more we must do to ensure that all students have this opportunity. Engaging students in learning about climate change—its causes, consequences, and solutions—across subjects and educational settings and developing their agency to act will show students how they can lead a more sustainable, resilient, and equitable future. We as educators can help them develop that agency and empower them for success.

Key Takeaways

1. Fostering an understanding of climate change—its causes, consequences, and solutions—is fundamental to helping students understand the world they will inherit.
2. Developing a foundational understanding of our relationship with our environment and our climate can begin at an early age and can be developed across subjects and educational settings.
3. Providing educators additional support, time, and preparation can help them in engaging students in learning about climate change.
4. Engaging students in deeper learning about climate change that is locally relevant and solutions-oriented can foster meaningful and empowering learning opportunities for students.
5. Recognizing common interests and shared values to support children and youth in building the understanding, knowledge, and skills they need for the future can help build community buy-in and support.

4

Supporting Students, Educators, and Schools in Adapting to Our Changing Climate

ON SEPTEMBER 20, 2017, *Hurricane Maria tore through Puerto Rico as a devastating category 4 storm with winds up to 155 miles per hour.*[1] *Maria came just weeks after Hurricane Irma, a category 5 storm, devastated the island. As a result of Hurricane Maria, thousands of people lost their lives, and many others had their livelihoods destroyed. Puerto Ricans were displaced from their homes, and schools were destroyed. Food, water, and other life essentials were scarce.*

In the wake of the storm, schools stayed closed for extended periods of time. The average student missed seventy-eight school days.[2] *Some schools closed permanently. Other schools sheltered community members when homes remained damaged and without power. Ninety-seven percent of roads were severely damaged, making services and supports hard to come by.*[3] *Many parents reported seeing increased anxiety, fear, and sadness among their children following the storm. Students had trouble concentrating in school when they were able to attend. Four in every five children with disabilities faced interruptions in their special education services, and many faced challenges accessing needed medication.*[4]

In the aftermath of the storm, many people and systems provided help to support students and families, and the rebuilding of schools. Dr. Victor Carrión, a professor and vice chair of psychiatry and behavioral sciences at Stanford University, traveled to Puerto Rico in partnership with the nonprofit Pure Edge, Inc. to accelerate the training of two thousand educators, social workers, and counselors to assist children with their mental health and their ability to cope with trauma.[5] *The US Department of Education provided $589 million through the RESTART Program to reopen schools and re-enroll students. This funding came on top of other federal funding from the Federal Emergency Management Agency (FEMA) to rebuild infrastructure.*

Even with the monetary and organizational aids, the school system and students have experienced lasting impacts of the hurricanes. While Puerto Rico's schools were already suffering from years of steady decline before Hurricane Maria, the decline was more dramatic for the 2017–2018 school year because of family displacement and other challenges. Nearly 40,000 of the 346,000 students left the school system—about an 11 percent decline in enrollment.[6] *As of fall 2021, student enrollment had dropped to 260,000 students, about 25 percent fewer students since before the hurricane.*

In September 2022, hundreds of schools suffered damage yet again and were forced to close due to Hurricane Fiona.[7] *Education reporter Kavitha Cardoza, in a piece for National Public Radio (NPR), wrote that "[i]n the 6th largest US district, natural disasters have disrupted learning for years."*[8] *In her reporting, she quotes an educator from the island: "2017 and 2022 children are not the same. . . . If you think about my seventh-graders right now, they've been going through something ever since second grade. So they have missed [out] on many, many opportunities to develop social, academic, behavioral, emotional skills." Cardoza emphasizes that Puerto Rico is "the canary in the coal mine that other districts could learn from as they grapple with the effects of climate change on learning, health and infrastructure."*[9]

While the experiences of students, families, and schools in Puerto Rico may seem extreme or distant to others across the country, they demonstrate how the increasingly intense consequences of a changing climate can have lasting and substantial effects. Scientists have made clear that, no matter how many mitigation strategies are deployed today, the planet will continue to get hotter in the coming decades.[10] A destabilized climate means weather will become more extreme. Schools across the country are already experiencing these impacts now.

The National Oceanic and Atmospheric Administration (NOAA) identified August 2023 as the hottest August on record.[11] Heat waves across the country collided with the start of the school year. Schools in New Jersey, Pennsylvania, Massachusetts, Illinois, Wisconsin, and Texas had to adjust schedules or in many cases cancel school.[12] Just a few months prior, at the end of the 2022–2023 school year, wildfire smoke from Canada descended on the East Coast, canceling outdoor recesses, sports practices, and end-of-year celebrations.[13] In September 2023, a rainstorm in New York City flooded over 150 school buildings.[14] Educators can wait for these events to occur, increasing the chances for more harmful impacts on health, learning, and infrastructure. Or they can use what is known about the likely effects of climate change now to prepare and adapt, making our communities more resilient to the impacts to come.

In this chapter, we describe the concepts of climate hazards and impacts, vulnerability and risks, and adaptation and resilience and what these concepts mean for students, educators, and schools. We outline key questions that educators should consider in preparing for climate effects and mind-sets to guide climate adaptation planning. We also highlight school districts utilizing adaptation mind-sets to prepare for, adapt to, and build resilience in a changing climate. Communities often face disruption first, prior to developing a plan. Rather than wait for disaster or disruption to strike, school districts can use the information we currently understand about our potential risks of climate change to create flexible and adaptable plans. While there will be aspects of adaptation beyond what we outline here, developing adaptation mind-sets can help leaders be flexible, prepared, and resilient for what's ahead.

CLIMATE ADAPTATION AND SCHOOLS

Climate change increases the frequency and severity of extreme weather.[15] In 2023, the United States experienced twenty-eight billion-dollar disasters, costing a total of $92.9 billion.[16] Hurricanes, wildfires, flooding, and extreme heat have impacted schools and communities around the country—a trend that will continue.

For students, climate change impacts their health, learning, and well-being. The ever-worsening effects of climate change take a toll on students' mental and physical health, as well as their opportunity to learn. At the school-systems level, climate change results in an increased number of weather-related school closures. The COVID-19 pandemic proved that public education systems need to be significantly more resilient in the face of disruption. The pandemic and the corresponding learning disruption exacerbated underlying inequities for students of color and low-income students. The impacts of climate change—from floods to heat waves, to wildfires—are disrupting schools across the country and similarly exacerbating inequities among the members of those communities. Schools do not exist in a vacuum; they are deeply connected to their communities. Community-level impacts—economic or social service disruption, trauma, and uncertainty—will also affect schools.

Climate models help us understand how climate change affects our communities. Educators can use this information to help empower protective action.[17] In particular, we can understand how the impacts of climate change differ depending on location. Schools in the West are more susceptible to wildfires and smoke, schools on the Gulf Coast are more likely to experience intense hurricanes, schools in the Southwest face extreme heat, and schools in the Midwest are more likely to see heavy rainfall and flooding.

Students, families, schools, and communities can advance solutions to buffer the effects on their community from climate change. For instance, a student with ties to caring and nurturing adults may be more resilient when coping with disruption. A school with a sustainable schoolyard helps to absorb excess stormwater, reducing flooding. A community with policies and supports to make people aware of and protected from the dangers of extreme heat, particularly for young children, can help keep community members safe and reduce heat-related illness. Planning for likely *climate risks* and *impacts* can help us *reduce our vulnerability, adapt,* and *build resilience.*

Climate Risks and Impacts

It is important to consider climate risks and impacts. Climate risks may include conditions like extreme heat, heavy precipitation, extended drought, and more intense hurricanes or wildfires. Climate impacts are how those hazards may affect us, nature, or our systems. Key to thinking about climate risks and impacts are heat, water, and drought. On average, climate change makes hot hotter, wet wetter, and dry dryer. This in turn affects air quality, the intensity of wildfires and hurricanes, exposure to infectious disease, food insecurity, and more. For instance, a risk like heavier rain may impact student learning if schools close due to flooding.

One of the most widespread risks of climate change is rising heat, which increases the number of excessively hot days each year. Communities across the country must live with this heat, and it is impacting our ways of living. For instance, young football players, with their heavier padding, experience more heat-related illness and even death.[18] Closures for heat days are becoming increasingly common in schools. One report found that more than 13,700 public schools that did not require cooling systems in 1970 now need them, and an additional 13,000 need heating, ventilation, and air-conditioning (HVAC) systems with better cooling capacity to keep up with the increased heat.[19]

The Baltimore City Schools (in Baltimore, Maryland) website, last updated August 31, 2022, lays out the following policy:

> The schools listed below will close or have early dismissal on extremely hot days, or that feel warmer due to a combination of heat and humidity. Schools *not* listed below have air-conditioning (but may dismiss early, if their systems require repair that cannot be completed within one day).[20]

About twenty schools included on this list do not have air conditioning or their air-conditioning is in need of repair. Our current warming from preindustrial levels averages just over 1°C. In climate models, at 1° warming, Baltimore experiences thirty-one days during the year on average with temperatures above 90°F, with the high end of the range being up to fifty-two days.[21] At 1.5°C warming, that average increases to thirty-six days and the high end of the range being fifty-eight days—nearly two months—of above 90°F weather. Yet many of the buildings where children and youth learn were not built to withstand this heat. They were built, like many in the northeastern United States, for a different climate, one that is fast disappearing.[22] Students, families, educators, and school leaders are either forced to close or to teach in uncomfortable conditions that are not conducive to learning and that are potentially unsafe.

Vulnerability and Risk

After considering risks and impacts, it is helpful to consider climate vulnerability and risk.[23] Vulnerability considers multiple factors to determine how susceptible a community is to suffering damage from a climate risk or impact. It is important to think about infrastructure quality, policies, resources, and community connectedness when considering vulnerability to risks. For instance, schools across the country without air conditioning are more vulnerable to impacts related to extreme heat, and students in those schools are more vulnerable to heat-related learning loss.

Climate risk focuses on the potential for negative consequences from risks and impacts. Risk incorporates hazards, impacts, vulnerability, and the likelihood of an occurrence. As the climate gets hotter, Baltimore is experiencing, on average, more hot days; that is, extreme heat is more likely to occur. Baltimore can assess the cost to students, families, schools, and the community: How will this increased probability result in school closures, impact student achievement and access to student supports and services, disrupt parents' and caregivers' ability to work, and exacerbate inequity? Considering both the probability of occurrence and the extent of potential loss will dictate the climate risk. If that risk is high, the community should consider opportunities to adapt and to reduce vulnerability and risk.[24]

Adaptation and Resilience

With an understanding of vulnerability and risk, a community can advance solutions to adapt and build resilience. Adapting means shifting what we do to reduce our vulnerability and risk. Several adaptation strategies can be evaluated related to a given climate risk. For instance, Baltimore could consider replacing outdated gas boilers with heat pumps that provide both heating and cooling, relocating students to other buildings on hot days, shifting to online learning, or providing additional instructional supports for students in these schools. These decisions are not as simple as they may appear, and each comes with trade-offs. For instance, how will these options impact the budget, transportation services, student learning, and the environment? Determining the best strategy depends on local needs, assets, and interests.

In addition to heat having an impact on teaching and learning in schools, our school infrastructure can also exacerbate the impacts of heat. Decisions around materials, landscaping, and infrastructure can contribute to heat island effects. A lack of trees in schoolyards or heat-trapping asphalt can create unsafe places for children to learn and play.

The Trust for Public Land, a national nonprofit, has partnered with the Oakland Unified School District (OUSD) to examine their schoolyard infrastructure. On an October day, Oakland students measured temperatures at a school playground at over 110°F, despite the mild temperature in the California Bay Area, as part of the project.[25] The principal said, "Right now it's like: concrete, concrete, concrete. . . . At recess I get kids crowded around the door to my office, because it's one of the only places on the yard with shade." Reducing the heat-trapping materials in our schools and schoolyard can be leveraged as an adaptation strategy.

The goal of adaptation is to help a community build resilience. A resilient community can prevent, respond to, and recover more effectively from climate risks and impacts. Adaptation and resilience should go hand in hand. Thinking about resilience without adaptation may result in less effective long-term strategies. For instance, building a wall around a school may initially prevent flooding, but it may not be a sufficient response. Fully recognizing the need to adapt may push a community to consider moving a school out of a floodplain altogether. Researchers have estimated that every $1 spent to prevent damage saves $6 in post-disaster recovery.[26]

Adapting and building resilience to climate impacts requires us to understand climate risk to students, schools, and communities and use that understanding to prepare and adjust. For school systems to adapt to a changing climate, school leaders, administrators, and educators must acknowledge the ways in which our climate is changing and how that change affects students, schools, and communities. To shift mind-sets toward adaptation and resilience, school leaders should consider the following questions.

Climate Adaptation Questions

- What are the likely climate risks and impacts for my school district?
- How might these climate risks and impacts affect:
  - Student learning and physical and mental health?

    - Schools' ability to engage students in learning and to provide support services?
    - Educators and school staff?
    - School infrastructure, building, grounds, and transportation?
    - Other systemic issues, like enrollment and budgets?
    - The broader community?
- What existing community assets can assist with adaptation and building resilience (such as municipal resilience planning or community-based organizations)?
- What steps can schools take to reduce vulnerability to climate risks, adapt, and build resilience?

Climate Adaptation Mind-Set

To have a climate adaptation mind-set, school leaders, administrators, and educators should:

- Understand climate risks and potential impacts for their community.
- Think strategically about how to prepare for instability.
- Make decisions to reduce vulnerability to climate risk and impacts.
- Partner with the broader community to support community-wide adaptation and resilience.
- Support students, educators, and the school community in understanding how to advance climate adaptation solutions.

Planning for uncertainty can be challenging, especially when there is a lot that may be out of schools' control. However, schools all over the country already experienced a significant period of uncertainty and disruption during the pandemic. Education leaders were forced to rethink how schools operated, teachers were forced to find creative ways to deliver content, and families had to cope with the unpredictable. Although schools are frequently considered slow to change, the pandemic demonstrated that schools can shift quickly. As we continue to learn lessons of what were effective shifts and ineffective shifts from the pandemic, and what students did and did not learn, one thing is certain: if we better prepare now for potential disruption, our students, families, communities, and schools will be better prepared to minimize disruption and cope with uncertainty.

ADAPTING BY CREATING RESILIENT SCHOOL SYSTEMS AND RESILIENT STUDENTS

> Because we are a coastal community prone to hurricanes, a coastal community prone to the arrival of literally dozens to thousands of children . . . we have naturally adapted to dealing with crises whether they are human crises, environmental crises or health crises.
>
> —Alberto Carvalho, former superintendent, Miami-Dade Public Schools[27]

After recognizing the potential harm of local climate disruptions, school districts can adapt and build more resilient school systems and teach students resiliency. Extreme weather can lead to lost learning days. Establishing policies to use virtual learning when students are unable to be in the building, which became common during the pandemic, can keep students connected and learning as an alternative to canceling school entirely. Districts that establish virtual learning as a resilience strategy should also consider digital and internet access as well as accessibility for students with disabilities to ensure that resilience strategies apply to all students.

To build resilience, schools should provide sufficient social emotional support for young people. Helping children and youth learn how to manage stress and develop strong relationships lays the foundation for them to become adults who are better prepared to cope with instability. "Children are not born being resilient," Dr. Victor Carrión noted. "They are actually vulnerable. That's why we take care of them. Resilience has to be built."[28] He added an essential element to building the resilience of young people: "strengthening of their support system." Schools can provide supportive mental health services for students before, during, and after extreme weather events.[29]

Even without directly experiencing the worst climate impacts themselves, 75 percent of young people in the United States have indicated a moderate to extreme level of worry about climate change.[30] Children and youth are witnessing the impacts of climate change, and many are experiencing eco-anxiety and persistent worries about their own futures and the prospects for future generations.[31]

Schools are integral to a support system for young people. Tiered supports, training more staff on eco-anxiety and trauma-informed practices, and partnerships with other districts can help increase a district's capacity to provide services even with counselor shortages.[32] Developing meaningful relationships with students and showing them that adults are working toward solutions can help reduce worry. Carrión said, "The first thing kids want to know is that they are secure, that they are safe. But also that those that are going to be taking care of them are competent and feel capable of providing that safety. That requires communication. . . . Children get empowered through knowledge."[33]

Miami-Dade County Public Schools

After being hit by category 5 Hurricane Andrew in 1992, Florida, and Miami-Dade County in particular, realized the urgency of extreme weather preparation. Many people were left homeless, and many of the county's schools were damaged by the storm and were closed for weeks.[34] After the storm, emergency management became a priority for the community and still remains integral to the mind-sets of community leaders today.[35] Creating policies to prepare for storms and flooding made the district more resilient and better able to deal with other disruptions. Years later, when the pandemic hit, Miami-Dade was able to shift to remote learning more effectively than other districts across the country because it had considered issues of technological access when thinking about storm preparedness.[36]

Facing multiple threats, including sea-level rise, more intense hurricanes, and heat, Miami-Dade has been called "ground zero" for climate change, and the county is actively taking steps to build its resilience.[37] The school district serves about 330,000 students each year—making it one of the largest school districts in the country. In addition to facing its own climate-related threats thanks to its location on the coast of Florida, Miami-Dade also recognizes the threats that nearby communities face and that may lead to displacement. As a result, it has put plans and systems in place to prepare for potential influxes of students.

In 2021, then superintendent of Miami-Dade County Public Schools (MDCPS), Alberto Carvalho (Carvalho now leads the Los Angeles Unified School District), spoke before the K12 Climate Action Commission to describe MDCPS's approach to supporting displaced students. He remarked, "It cannot be ignored that our location in South Florida provides ample opportunities to execute processes and procedures to prepare for the climate change that our entire globe is experiencing."[38]

MDCPS applied a three-tiered approach for supporting displaced students, with each tier depending on the number of students arriving to the district. These support systems focused specifically on meeting the students' academic, physical health, mental health, and social emotional needs. Carvalho described the goals of these procedures: "to minimize the bureaucratic process for student enrollment [and] the certification for teachers who may come from areas like Puerto Rico." The district wanted to ensure enrollment and certification processes were "accelerated and expedited." MDCPS enrollment policies and approaches included the following:

- *Smaller influx of students*: With a smaller number of students where the influx is "steady, but slow," the district worked to support enrollment within schools across the county. It focused on interviewing students along with their parents or guardians quickly and evaluating the students to determine what, if any, English language supports or special education supports and services might be necessary. As Carvalho noted, the district wants to make sure that "the intervention and the acceleration toward learning potential [are] in place."

- *Moderate influx of students*: If the district experienced a moderate influx of students, it needs to build its capacity to support that enrollment. The district does this by establishing one to three enrollment centers to register students. It partners with other agencies in the county, like the department of health, to ensure that students have any needed immunizations or other health supports. The enrollment centers can be more comprehensive, allowing for "integration in the system in a faster way."
- *Large influx of students*: The final policy Carvalho described occurred if the district received hundreds to thousands of students per week. In this case, it would establish a full-service school to support students because this approach would support the students' integration into the school system most effectively and efficiently.

In these extreme circumstances, teachers, in addition to students, may be forced to leave their communities as well. In the aftermath of Hurricane Maria, MDCPS also sought to help displaced teachers in getting certification expeditiously. These teachers, often from the same communities as displaced students, shared a connection to the culture and experience, which was an asset in efforts to support students. In these circumstances, it is necessary, as Carvalho noted, to "cut through the red tape."

The number of people forced to leave their homes and communities because of climate-related impacts is projected to increase in the years to come, both here in the United States and around the globe.[39] Shifts in response to a specific weather event or the cascading impacts of climate on issues like housing affordability, food insecurity, or political instability may force families to move and seek opportunities to regain stability in their lives. As a result, school districts in the United States will experience enrollment shifts: potential upticks in areas like Miami-Dade and potential enrollment declines like in Puerto Rico. Students and families who are forced to relocate are likely arriving in new areas after experiencing trauma and loss. Academic, social, emotional, and mental health needs are critically important for incoming students, and yet these come with a cost as well. Superintendent Carvalho shared, "To us, both sides of the coin are important." He explained that academic preparation needs to be "side by side with social emotional support and mental health support, considering the trauma that these children arrived with after living through a hurricane disruption or an earthquake in Haiti."

Miami-Dade continues to experience shifts in enrollment. In 2023, MDCPS experienced a larger increase in enrollment than that after Hurricane Maria: twenty thousand new students immigrated to the district over the school year, and they came from places across Latin America, spurred by economic hardships, political instability, and violence.[40] The effects of climate instability outside the United States can have domestic repercussions, too. For instance, the Central American Dry Corridor acts as a "risk multiplier," further exacerbating and igniting poverty, instability, and violence in the region, and has led to the migration and increased enrollment of Central American students in MDCPS and US schools.[41] While MDCPS has plans and structures to support student enrollment and English language development, these influxes of students, along with teacher shortages and budgetary constraints, strain the district's ability to provide needed supports effectively.[42]

School districts must plan now to prepare for disruptions, shifts in enrollment, trauma, anxiety, and loss and how all such changes may impact their school system, students, educators, and community. It has become increasingly important to recognize our broader connections to each other, across communities, and among different school districts. Building relationships with nearby school districts can help better prepare communities for potential disruptions. State and federal policy makers should help districts build resilience to support all students in the decades to come. While we cannot entirely predict where or when a certain climate risk may upend our home or our community and force displacement, we can recognize that we are part of a broader community, and schools can play a vital role in supporting children, youth, and families.

ADAPTING BY ENHANCING COMMUNITY RESILIENCE

> When everything else is shut down from these extreme climate events, we need our schools to have the lights on. We need those kitchens to keep working, so that we can continue to feed kids and families.
>
> —Laura Capps, former school board member, Santa Barbara Unified School District[43]

Whether you are an educator, leader, or policy maker, you should consider the opportunity for schools to adapt and be better prepared for the worst impacts of climate change. This can also help schools serve as community hubs of climate resilience. Schools are already foundational pillars of their communities. In many cases, they provide access to food, health care, and social services to students and families. When schools are equipped to retain critical functions in extreme weather, they can deliver essential services and shelter community members.

When school grounds are adapted to reduce heat and flooding, it also reduces heat and flooding for the local community. Acknowledging that community benefit can help schools secure resources and support for climate adaptation work. As we mentioned previously, schools contribute to heat island effects for an entire community, and schools and communities alike are more susceptible to flooding when their schoolyard is covered in asphalt. Chicago Public Schools (CPS) partnered with the Chicago Department of Water Management and the Metropolitan Water Reclamation District of Greater Chicago, plus two nonprofits, the Healthy Schools Campaign and Openlands, to address asphalt schoolyards across the city.[44] Heavier rainfall left Chicago experiencing more frequent storm-related flooding. To reduce flooding, these partners transitioned Chicago's impermeable asphalt schoolyards to permeable green spaces. The school district leveraged resources across the capital partners to develop the sustainable schoolyards in collaboration with the community and created healthy places for students to learn and play. This had the added benefit of retaining stormwater runoff. Thus far, the new partnership—Space to Grow®—has changed playgrounds at over thirty schools, retained a significant amount of rainwater, and engaged students outdoors. When education leaders understand how their schools can benefit broader local climate adaptation efforts, they can seek partnerships with their municipalities to create more resilient communities.

Santa Barbara Unified School District

In 1969, an oil well erupted off the coast of Santa Barbara County. Massive amounts of oil and tar washed up on the Santa Barbara beaches. Oil and tar remained even three years later, despite massive cleanup efforts. Laura Capps was born in 1972, but she vividly remembers the polluted beach. As a child, she would leave the beach with her feet covered not in sand but in tar. Her mother kept a bottle of lighter fluid handy to break through the grease and rinse her feet upon returning home. Going to the beach would normally be a joyful memory, and for Laura, it sits juxtaposed to this memory of environmental damage.

This oil spill spurred action in the larger environmental movement, and Laura had a front seat to that movement's development. It fostered her own desire for protecting the environment. As an adult, Laura moved back to Santa Barbara to advocate for local action as president for an environmental nonprofit. Driving around Santa Barbara, Laura recalled noticing how visible the schools were in her community and yet how few of them used renewable energy. She noted, "When you drive around, you live in your neighborhood, or you bike or walk, and you look up [at schools] and see that there was no solar, even though we lived in such a conducive climate." Laura recognized that schools, as central in the community, could be a lever for change. Armed with this knowledge, in 2016, she won a seat on the Santa Barbara Unified School District (SBUSD) board.

SBUSD serves about thirteen thousand students across twenty-one schools, with slightly more than 50 percent of the students enrolled in Santa Barbara schools coming from low-income families.[45] Early in her tenure, Laura pushed the board to adopt renewable energy, but her efforts were met with resistance. This was not ideological resistance against the concept of renewable energy; it was resistance based in priorities. SBUSD grappled with too many competing issues already, and the board was not ready to prioritize renewable energy. As Laura described, other board members indicated support, but "not let's put this at the top of the list."

In December 2017, the Thomas wildfire burned much of the hillsides in Santa Barbara. About 280,000 acres destroyed over 1,000 buildings.[46] At the time, the wildfire broke records as the largest in California's recent history. (In the years since, it has been surpassed by a half dozen larger fires.) The impacts of wildfires are not isolated to the fire itself. The debris and damage to the soil after a wildfire is extinguished leave the land especially prone to dangerous mudslides and flooding.[47] In January 2018, Santa Barbara County experienced torrential rain followed by destructive mudslides. Twenty-three people died, homes were damaged and destroyed, and power outages forced evacuations. The community struggled with the impacts, and in the aftermath, it had a new appreciation for the need to build community resilience in preparation for extreme weather events.

The community's vulnerability, along with the economic argument about saving money on utilities, helped bring the school board together to adopt a plan to install solar panels and batteries to create microgrids at several schools across the district. These microgrids help provide power and shelter to the community in the event of outages, storms, and mudslides. In 2022, the district had installed enough solar across fourteen different school sites to generate 94 to 98 percent of the electricity demand.[48] Six of these locations are also secured with battery storage to store the renewable energy and thus keep the lights on during outages. The district used a power purchase agreement to cover the costs associated with installation, and the twenty-eight-year agreement is projected to save the district about $7.8 million on energy costs during the lifetime of the agreement.[49] Plus the community, in building its resilience, is better protected from devastating disruption.

There was some initial worry about how neighbors might feel about the visual changes, with large solar panels covering the front of school buildings or canopies on school campuses. But the community has been largely receptive. Community members recognize the benefits of students being able to see the solar panels or have a shadier spot to eat lunch. Laura acknowledged the latter being especially important "with our rising temperatures."

With the solar microgrid plan adopted, SBUSD began taking sustainability more seriously, but Laura mentioned the importance of ensuring that this work didn't "just fall to the wayside." The district made the decision to hire a sustainability director, who was integral in the execution of the plan and in ensuring that issues of sustainability "get addressed and consistently."

Laura's advice to others embarking on this work is "start with community" rather than "just trying to forge ahead solo." This work requires considerable collaboration and finding allies, especially with students, which can provide effective conditions to advance meaningful action. Students helped collect over one thousand signatures in support of SBUSD's work. This enabled students to "be engaged in something and now they can see the end product."

Laura has moved on from the school board and now serves as an elected Santa Barbara County supervisor, but she still relies on schools to recognize the critical role they play in community resilience. When California faced torrential atmospheric rivers at the beginning of 2023 and their highways closed, one of Laura's first calls was to the school superintendent. She remarked, "Our schools are safe havens."

CONCLUSION

The worsening effects of climate change are becoming increasingly apparent in the work of educators. Learning disruptions or lost learning, health impacts, heat, enrollment shifts, and emotional stress affect educators, students, families, and communities. But schools have the opportunity to advance climate solutions, harness what we know about likely impacts, be better prepared for impacts to come, and help communities adapt. Schools are essential actors in helping our communities lead a more resilient future.

Key Takeaways

1. Climate change impacts schools across the country now, and adapting can make us more resilient to challenges to come.
2. Education leaders should consider local climate risks and vulnerabilities as well as community assets to develop effective adaptation and resilience strategies.
3. In developing adaptation plans, education leaders should consider strategies to support student learning and mental and physical health.
4. Education leaders should recognize the vital role that schools play in community resilience and seek broader partnerships, whether with another agency, municipality, or a nearby school district. This can help increase resources and support for climate adaptation and resilience.

5

Supporting Schools in Mitigating Their Carbon Pollution

***IN 2017, DR. MICHAEL HESTER** was in his first year as superintendent in Batesville, Arkansas. Working with his school board, he wanted to prove himself with ambitious and aligned strategic goals for the district. After workshopping the plan, they settled on four strategic goals: (1) student achievement, (2) attracting and retaining teachers, (3) efficiency, and (4) partnerships.*

As a district, Batesville was facing financial challenges. Hester was tasked with finding "efficiencies" in the budget to get the district back on track—a difficult issue to tackle because the choices about what areas of the budget to cut are always hard. Hester commented, "In education, you get what you get." He knew they needed to "create money in the budget." Hester recognized an opportunity to think about the budget and "efficiencies" differently. Rather than focusing on what to cut, Hester and his team realized the potential for the district to create income. Arkansas State Act 464 established net metering, which essentially allows owners of renewable energy systems to get credit for the energy they generate and provide to the grid—a policy common to the vast majority of states.[1] Hester saw this as "a rare opportunity" for a school system.

If they built a solar array, the district could "create money" in their budget by receiving the credit from the generation of energy. The money that they had been spending on energy to power their buildings could be redirected toward their core strategic priorities: improving student achievement and attracting and retaining teachers. As they embarked on their plan to build a solar array, they understood they would need to rely heavily on their fourth strategic priority and develop meaningful partnerships, including with the community.

Like every aspect of our society, schools contribute to carbon emissions that impact our environment. Schools require considerable resources to serve 50 million students annually across the country. These resource demands align with the primary drivers of our country's emissions: energy, transportation, buildings, and food. The nearly 100,000 K–12 public schools in the United States are one of the largest energy consumers in the public sector: they operate the largest mass-transit fleet in the country with 480,000 school buses, and they serve over 7 billion meals annually with related food waste.[2]

To mitigate our impact on climate change, our entire society must decarbonize (reduce) carbon pollution that contributes to the warming of the planet. For the education sector to decarbonize, schools must think differently about how they get power, heat and cool buildings, take students to and from school, source food, and dispose of waste. The process of decarbonization takes time.[3] If decarbonization becomes a priority in decision making, we create significant benefits, including reduced annual operations costs, improved health and well-being, and firsthand learning experiences for students with the technologies that will power the future.

In this chapter, we highlight the opportunity for schools to reduce carbon pollution and school districts to use mitigation mind-sets, and in this way lead efforts to transition to clean renewable energy, improve building sustainability, shift to electric school buses, and promote sustainable food use. School districts seeking to reduce their carbon pollution may benefit from an emissions assessment to determine their greatest needs and opportunities to decarbonize fully. While there will likely be aspects of decarbonization beyond what we outline here (for instance, decisions about waste disposal), the strategies we provide, starting with energy, buildings, transportation, and food, will help school districts make significant progress.

THE OPPORTUNITY TO REDUCE CARBON POLLUTION

Many likely have had the experience of driving near a yellow school bus and seeing the dark clouds of smoke pouring out of the bus's tailpipe. Diesel pollution is just one example of an environmental hazard that can have significant impacts on student health and learning.[4] Poor indoor air quality and unhealthy food are two others. Transitioning to electric school buses reduces air pollution because electric buses do not have diesel tailpipe emissions. Updating heating, ventilation, and air-conditioning (HVAC) systems to high-performance electric systems can improve indoor air quality at schools.[5] These strategies reduce the risks of asthma in children and improve attendance.[6] Such methods do more than decrease pollution risk; they have educational benefits, too. When schools serve healthy food, including locally grown sustainable food, students learn about nutrition and develop healthier eating habits.[7] Educators can use school infrastructure and sustainability improvements to teach students about clean energy, composting, electric vehicles, and more, thus enabling them to be better prepared to support our larger societal efforts for decarbonization.

Rethinking these processes to decarbonize schools may seem like a daunting task, especially when so much of our lives have depended on fossil fuels, but school districts across the country are demonstrating the multiple benefits to schools in doing this work. Tim Cole, the former sustainability manager for Virginia Beach City Public Schools in Virginia, referred to the benefits of reducing emissions and advancing sustainability in schools as an opportunity to make progress on the "triple bottom line," or social, environmental, and economic outcomes.[8] Whether someone supports these initiatives because of the improved social, economic, or environmental outcomes, these efforts create an opportunity to bring people together. Recognizing these benefits, school districts are making ambitious commitments, including Boston's Green New Deal for Public Schools and New York City's efforts to shift schools to all-electric heating.[9] Rather than being one additional thing for schools to do, these strategies can be critical in making progress across strategic priorities, promoting student learning, and benefiting school districts financially.

There is also no better time than the present to make these improvements thanks to the resources and support from the federal government. The Infrastructure Investment and Jobs Act (IIJA) includes a grant program from the Environmental Protection Agency (EPA) to support schools in transitioning to electric school buses.[10] The first round of funding was announced in the summer of 2022. The EPA received such a high number of applicants that they doubled the initial round of funding from $500 million to $1 billion, awarding rebates to four hundred school districts across the country.[11] The Inflation Reduction Act (IRA) offers tax credits and grants to support schools in shifting to renewable energy and clean transportation and improving building efficiency.[12] These tax credits could save school districts up to 50 to 60 percent on the upfront costs of installing renewable energy, including ground-source heat pumps, on-site solar, and energy storage.

Those working within the climate field generally refer to emissions as scope 1, scope 2, and scope 3 emissions:[13]

1. Scope 1 emissions are carbon emissions that are generated on the school site under school control. Scope 1 emissions might come from systems like furnaces, water heaters, gas stoves, or school buses.

2. Scope 2 emissions are not generated directly on-site, but they are the emissions associated with electricity used to power the building.
3. Scope 3 emissions are not produced directly by the school; they are indirectly related to schools. An example are the emissions related to how teachers get to and from school in vehicles not owned by the school.

It's helpful for school districts looking to reduce carbon pollution to understand how their emissions fit in this frame.

Reducing carbon pollution requires us to change how schools use energy, buildings, transportation, and food. For school systems to decarbonize, school leaders, administrators, educators, and staff members must change the ways in which our school systems operate. To shift mind-sets toward decarbonization, school leaders should consider the following questions to put them on a path toward net zero over time.

Climate Mitigation Questions

- What are the main sources of carbon pollution in my district across energy, buildings, transportation, food, and waste?
- How can my district reduce these emissions in a strategic and equity-centered way, where we prioritize under-resourced schools that can benefit the most?
- Do we have policies in place that prioritize reducing carbon pollution (for instance, a policy ensuring that when a building system needs replacement, it is replaced with modern fossil-fuel-free technology)?
- Are we providing opportunities for students to learn about climate solutions firsthand?

Climate Mitigation Mind-Set

To have a climate mitigation mind-set, school leaders need to:

- Understand the sources of carbon pollution for a school district.
- Prevent additional carbon pollution in new actions.

- Think strategically to reduce existing carbon pollution in a way that prioritizes underserved schools and communities.
- Support students, educators, and the school community in understanding how to advance climate mitigation solutions.

REDUCING CARBON POLLUTION FROM BUILDINGS AND ENERGY

> Generally the building doesn't cost more to do these [net-zero energy] features . . . if you are smart about how you do it.
>
> —Jeff Chambers, the director of design and construction for Arlington Public Schools, Virginia[14]

Buildings and energy combined account for over 40 percent of US carbon emissions.[15] To help school systems get to net-zero greenhouse gas emissions, they must reduce carbon pollution related to their buildings and energy use. This can be done at the point of new construction, during building retrofits and modernization, at the end of life for major building systems, or during the installation of new renewable energy systems.

Underinvestment in America's schools, by an estimated $85 billion annually, has a negative impact on energy efficiency, health, and learning.[16] In 2021, our schools received a D+ on America's infrastructure report card.[17] A 2020 US Government Accountability Office (GAO) report found that 54 percent of districts need to replace at least two building systems, for example, HVAC, in many of their schools.[18] The underinvestment is worse for communities of color and low-income communities. As a result, aging infrastructure and higher maintenance costs often prevent underserved communities from affording the upfront costs needed to improve school infrastructure.[19] Aging infrastructure also means schools require more energy to operate buildings. In many districts across the country, energy costs are a significant portion of the annual budget, the second highest cost, second only to salaries.[20]

The need to modernize school infrastructure to contend with extreme weather and achieve climate goals is an opportunity to address long-standing inequities in student access to healthy learning environments, and these learning environments are where our children spend more of their waking hours.[21] Creating opportunities for schools, in particular those in under-resourced communities, to improve their buildings can help advance equity, create healthier spaces, improve learning, free monies in the budget for teaching and learning, and reduce our impact on the environment.

Building New? Aim for Zero

If a school district is building a new school, it can use the opportunity to build a net-zero energy school. Net-zero energy schools produce as much clean energy as they consume and have especially high benefits for both the environment and school budgets.[22] According to the US Department of Energy's National Renewable Energy Lab (NREL), net-zero schools can cost less to build and operate than conventional school designs.[23] As of 2019, eleven states had at least one public K–12 net-zero school, as identified by the New Buildings Institute (NBI), and seventeen states had at least one public K–12 school that was considered net-zero energy emerging.[24]

Education leaders can leverage multiple strategies to achieve net-zero energy. Thinking about building design to minimize energy consumption is a critical first step. Then schools should consider the opportunity to use renewable energy to meet their energy needs. The energy intensity of the building is essential to achieve net-zero status. The energy intensity of the building is measured by energy use intensity (EUI). When starting new construction, districts can focus on lowering the energy intensity of the building with decisions about insulation, building location, indoor air quality, and more. These decisions can reduce the overall energy demand for a building, which in turn reduces the amount of renewable energy needed to offset the building's energy use. One of the most important decisions that district leaders can make is choosing architecture and building engineering partners with experience designing high-performance, net-zero buildings.

Arlington Public Schools

Arlington Public Schools in Virginia, outside Washington, DC, is a midsize school district, serving about 27,500 students in thirty-five schools and five programs. About 44 percent of the student population is white, 29 percent Latino, 10.5 percent Black, and 8.5 percent Asian. Their mission is "to ensure all students learn and thrive in safe, healthy, and supportive learning environments."[25]

Arlington built its first net-zero elementary school, Discovery Elementary School, in 2015. It had not originally intended to build a net-zero school, but the architects suggested the possibility. When they demonstrated that it could be accomplished within their budget, Arlington agreed. After seeing the annual budgetary savings, along with the learning benefits, from Discovery, Arlington continued to work with VMDO Architects and CMTA (a consulting engineering firm that specializes in mechanical, electrical, and plumbing design) and built two additional net-zero schools.

Alice West Fleet Elementary School opened in 2019 and is set to become one of the largest net-zero schools in the country. During a visit to Alice West Fleet, Wyck Knox, a lead architect for the building, proudly acknowledged that Alice West Fleet is "an all-electric building" and "no fossil fuels are burned to operate the building."[26] The building was designed with the intention of being net zero. Decisions about the building envelope and the position of the building on the lot to maximize the south-facing roof for solar generation were essential to help the school achieve net-zero status. The building has 1,532 solar panels that produce 728,900 kWh of energy per year, and seventy-two geothermal pipes help heat and cool the building. To help guide the decisions, they incorporated principles from the Leadership in Energy and Environmental Design (LEED) rating system and the WELL Building Standard to ensure the health and sustainability of the learning environment.

This building is not simply about the energy design features; rather, it is a place of learning, and the sustainability mission is infused in what students learn. At the entrance of the building is a pole, dubbed the "power pole." It has blue lights that indicate the amount of energy the building is producing with features like the solar panels on the roof; red lights indicate the amount of energy being consumed. Students engage in conversations about how things like a stormy day might impact energy generation or how turning off all the lights in the school impacts energy consumption. The solar panels are visible from classroom windows, and while learning about bar graphs in math, students graph the energy production from the school. Monique O'Grady, an Arlington School board member who joined the tour, highlighted this learning: "These students are learning more than just what's in the books. They are changing their hearts and minds and thoughts for the future."

System Replacements and Retrofits Can Support Decarbonization

While many net-zero energy schools are built new and while the number of net-zero energy schools continues to increase across the country, retrofitting buildings or replacing building systems can help existing schools significantly reduce emissions and approach net-zero status. Schools can implement big and small changes related to scope 1 and scope 2 emissions to decrease their reliance on fossil fuels and support decarbonization related to scope 1 and scope 2 emissions. Such changes include infrastructure improvements to reduce air leakage, installing geothermal (that is, ground-source) or air-source heat pumps, replacing inefficient windows, and adding LED lighting. For instance, replacing old fossil-fuel-dependent building systems with high-performance, electrified building systems (including geothermal or air-source heat pumps or induction stovetops) can eliminate on-site scope 1 emissions. Energy efficiency retrofits, like replacing windows, or education to support educators, staff members, and students in conserving energy can reduce the amount of electricity needed from the grid (scope 2 emissions).

HVAC systems, in particular, account for over half of schools' energy use each year, and 61 percent of those HVAC units burn fossil fuels on-site to operate.[27] HVAC systems help schools with ventilation (moving air in and out), filtration (removing polluted air), and conditioning (keeping building temperatures comfortable). Rather than relying on fossil fuels, modern heat pumps remove heat from the air, the water, or the ground to operate. These systems are more efficient, meaning in addition to reducing carbon pollution, they also help save money. In Berkeley County Schools in West Virginia, seven schools installed geothermal heating and cooling systems and made additional energy efficiency upgrades. This shift resulted in a 75 percent decrease in energy use in those schools and saved the district an estimated $1.7 million annually.[28]

Getting Power from the Sun

Adding renewable energy can help schools reduce their carbon pollution related to electricity use. Solar-powered schools are growing in popularity across the country. About 8,400 K–12 schools in the United States have installed solar panels as of 2021, more than double the number of schools with solar in 2014.[29] Yet there is still a significant opportunity to increase its use because less than 10 percent of schools in the United States currently use solar energy. With sizable roofs, parking lots, or open spaces, schools have huge potential to install solar panels on their property. On-site solar can be developed through either new construction or retrofitting existing buildings. Solar panels can be mounted on a roof or over a parking lot, or they can be used to provide shade in an open space. When installed together, solar panels with sufficient battery storage create microgrids, which have the added benefit of building community resilience. With a microgrid, like those in the Santa Barbara Unified School District (SBUSD) discussed in chapter 4, community members can come to the school to plug in or cool off in the event of power outages.

Batesville School District in Arkansas

The Batesville School District in Arkansas serves about 3,500 students across seven schools. Their mission is to "empower today's students for tomorrow's challenges." Dr. Michael Hester served as superintendent from 2017 to 2024 and collaborated with the school board, educators, and the community to build a large solar array for the district.

Batesville's shift to renewable energy started with a look at efficiencies and an interest in building high-quality partnerships. Hester remarked, "You've got to have the right partner in energy, and then you've got to have the right legislation." Arkansas State Act 464 put in place legislation that enabled the district to generate income, and they had the opportunity to partner with an energy company Entegrity who could support them through the process, starting with an energy audit. The audit revealed the high cost of their existing energy use as well as the potential to transition to renewable energy. They could pay for the solar installation over time with their annual savings, and they estimated that the new system would save them $4 million over twenty years. With a performance contract, they would have no upfront costs and little risk because the contract guaranteed the savings. They would not be on the hook if the savings did not pan out.

Hearing the potential of creating money within their budget, the motivation for Hester to support the project was easy. He knew firsthand the strain educators face financially. "I was a teacher. I had to work three jobs to survive." He made a commitment to himself that when he was in an administrative position, he would do what he could to support educators because they are the key to helping students succeed. "The most important thing we can do is take care of our teachers who take care of our kids." He added, "To put students first. It starts with who you put with those kids." This could be an opportunity to increase teacher pay. "We were looking for efficiencies and partners in our quest, and then we took the money to attract and retain staff."

With the plan in mind, leaders in Batesville worked to build buy-in with the community, starting with the staff members. "If you don't have grassroots buy-in, then that's not going to continue to grow," Hester noted. While there may have been resistance, Hester tied the initiative to the instructional mission and salaries. "When we said, we're gonna apply it to salaries you know they're listening." The staff recognized the potential for the solar project as well. This would not be a come-and-go initiative for the school district; it would create the opportunity to reinvest in them and their core work.

The school district leaders held about thirty town hall meetings to explain the project, get feedback, ensure receptivity, and "be transparent with families about the changes." In explaining the project, they knew it was important to ground the conversation in shared values. They understood that people in the community had a deep appreciation for nature and wanted to protect the natural world. "We love our clean water, our beautiful trees and mountains, and the beautiful Delta with the Mississippi River," Hester remarked. "When you talk about taking care of the environment, people have a love of the outdoors here."

But the environmental benefits were not the only argument that won the community over. "We're a conservative state. Conservatives love that you're maximizing your tax dollars and saving money, and when we talk about how we could do this it would pay for itself, and we would not raise taxes. That was our talking point."

With the support from the community, Batesville built a solar array with 1,483 solar panels. The move to solar power cut their monthly energy bill by nearly 75 percent. They also took other energy-saving measures, including transitioning to LED lighting, replacing HVAC units and windows, and installing centrally controlled thermostats. The solar array was completed in 2019, and with these other energy-saving measures, it saved $362,100 that year.[30] These savings went into teacher pay, increasing salaries up to $9,000 per year.[31]

The array does more than generate energy. It is also integrated with the curriculum, supported in part by a grant from their partner Entegrity. They have a solar track curriculum where teachers can learn how to connect the solar array to student learning in math and science classes. They also leveraged the opportunity to create a career pathway to connect students to clean energy jobs. "They have it in our backyard, literally. [They] can go out and look at how the mechanics work and then learn how the math and science is applied." Megan Renihan, Batesville's communication director, added that, with this exposure, maybe the students will consider careers in clean energy. "I want to be the one that designs that solar panel, or I want to be the one that comes up with the next energy efficient way to apply that." They emphasize with students, "These are the types of jobs that will be available to you in the future."

There are still challenges ahead. Hester worries that Arkansas State Act 464 could get changed or watered down, and a bill passed in 2023 does cut the reimbursement rate. But there is growing interest in solar across their state, and the coalition of people supporting renewable energy will continue to push forward. The district is focused on what's next, how it can build a bigger system, and how it might be able to get electric school buses that can be powered by solar energy. With all the benefits of the initiative, one thing Hester is extremely proud of: "We went from worst to first in our area on our salaries."

REDUCING CARBON POLLUTION FROM SCHOOL TRANSPORTATION

> It's very complicated, but sustainability is the kind of work you should be spending your time on.
>
> —Gilbert Blue Feather Rosas, Modesto City Schools, California

Transportation accounts for about 28 percent of our country's emissions.[32] Students get to and from school many different ways: biking, walking, public transportation, school buses, and private cars. These options have different emissions impacts. Communities can reduce transportation emissions associated with students' commutes to school; however, alternative options may be more or less feasible depending on each community's location. Where feasible, city-led efforts to increase safe routes to school for walking and biking can support alternative, emissions-free methods of transportation.

Sam Balto, a physical education teacher in Portland, Oregon, went viral for the bike bus he created.[33] On Wednesdays, Balto would wear a neon vest; play music; and, along with other parent volunteers, caravan about 170 students on bikes to school. In addition to being fun, this bike caravan has brought the community together; reduced pollution and traffic; increased physical activity for the students; and provided an opportunity to talk about climate change, emissions related to transportation, and solutions.

One of the most common ways students get to and from school is on a school bus. About 57 percent of public school students rode on school buses in the 2018–2019 school year.[34] Many of us have had the experience of riding on a big yellow school bus, or we have seen them on the streets in our communities or depicted on television shows, including *The Magic School Bus*. The big yellow school bus is ingrained in our culture. In fact, with 480,000 buses nationwide, school buses are the largest mass transit fleet in the country.[35] Currently, about 90 percent of school buses run on diesel fuel.[36]

The tailpipe emissions from diesel-powered buses contribute to climate change, create air pollution, and harm student health and well-being. These emissions have been shown to have a negative impact on academic performance and increase absenteeism.[37] Students from Black households, low-income students, and students with disabilities are more likely to ride school buses to and from school, which increases their exposure to polluted air.[38] And young children in particular are more likely to experience negative impacts on their respiratory, cardiovascular, and neurological systems.[39]

School districts transitioning from diesel-powered buses to electric school buses can see substantial environmental, economic, and health benefits. Electric school buses run on electricity rather than gas and eliminate polluting tailpipe emissions. In addition to the absence of fumes, the electric bus rides tend to be both smoother and quieter than a diesel bus. To minimize all greenhouse gas emissions connected to bus transportation, it's important to think beyond the bus route, too. School districts can explore options for charging infrastructure and power electric buses with clean renewable energy like solar.

Costs associated with electric school buses and the needed charging infrastructure frequently pose a barrier. The upfront costs for an electric bus can be nearly three times as high as that for a diesel bus, but federal programs are increasing the affordability of these vehicles. Tax credits in the IRA can reduce the cost of the bus up to $40,000. The Clean School Bus (CSB) Program and Clean Heavy-Duty Vehicles (CHDV) Program from the EPA offer funding to offset costs associated with electric buses, workforce training, and charging infrastructure. Once in operation in a district, electric school buses save money: an estimated $2,000 in fuel costs and $4,400 in maintenance costs annually.[40] During its lifetime, an electric school bus's projected savings can reach $170,000 in maintenance and fuel costs.

Some school districts have leveraged public-private partnerships to afford the transition to electric school buses. Montgomery County Public Schools (MCPS) in Maryland has developed a plan to transition its entire bus fleet to electric through a partnership with Highland Electric Fleets. Highland leases the buses to MCPS at a rate similar to the district's costs for purchasing and maintaining a diesel bus, thus reducing the challenge of higher upfront costs for the district. Highland makes a profit over time with the reduced costs to maintain and operate an electric fleet. The district anticipates having 326 electric buses on the road by 2025 and a fully electric fleet in ten years. School board president Brenda Wolff commented about the partnership: "Moving to electric transportation is not only a necessary response to climate change, but it is also something students have asked for at Board of Education meetings. Partnerships with organizations like Highland are so important. It allows us to demonstrate our commitment to becoming a more sustainable organization while defraying the high upfront cost of electric school buses."[41]

Find the Funding: Stockton Unified School District and Modesto City Schools

Gilbert Blue Feather Rosas had spent much of his career in the private sector, where he felt autonomy to shake things up. In 2012, he entered the public sector as an energy manager for Stockton Unified School District (SUSD) in California and described the shift as "a real culture shock." He realized he had to work within the existing system, and his job was saving the school money on water, energy, and gas. To do so, he implemented strategies like the student energy patrol. He pushed himself and others in the district to consider the school building more like one might consider their home. He would remind people that they wouldn't just leave all the lights on at home because that would affect their monthly energy bills. The same thing applies to schools too.

Once the savings started to appear, Gil investigated more ways to save. He learned more about sustainability and the US Department of Education Green Ribbon Schools (ED-GRS) program, which highlighted schools across the country making strides on energy conservation. He discovered an opportunity to transition to electric school buses through grants from the California Air Resources Board (CARB) and the California Energy Commission (CEC), and rebates from the local utility company.

Less than a year after submitting the first grant proposal, the district built charging stations and had its first set of electric buses on the road. These buses save the district money on operations and maintenance and help students breathe cleaner air. Gil's philosophy had been to build a charging station for twenty-four buses, even though their first purchase included only eleven. He led with: "How do we maximize our efforts once you dig up that trench?" He wanted to make sure they wouldn't have charging as a barrier later as they secured more buses. He also ensured that those charging stations were powered by the sun.

Gil shifted to Modesto City Schools (MCS) to then lead the transition of their bus fleet. He described Modesto as "all in." The superintendent, school board, and staff were committed. With their first purchase, Modesto secured thirty electric school buses, enough to transition half their fleet.

Seeing the benefits of sustainability for students, the environment, and the budget, Gil recognized that this has "just become a passion" for him. Now he is asking questions at Modesto to get students more engaged: How can we expose students to career pathways in sustainability? How can we engage them in learning about solutions? He started with having his own grandson shadow him on the job over the summer. His grandson had not landed on a career to pursue. He knew he didn't want to be in an office and had thought of construction as one of the only jobs available to him to be outside and to use his hands. After shadowing Gil, he saw a range of careers from which he could choose. He currently has his sights on electrical engineering. Gil emphasized the importance of showing and promoting these different green job pathways. He also acknowledged the importance of people of color (like him) acting as models for students. "I'm looking at business, nobody looks like me, so to see people that look like you—I think that's very important for students."

Gil has faced challenges with people buying into his work, the biggest being the speed with which a district can move. His response: "I just keep going through it." How does he keep pushing through? "Turning those frowns upside down and saying, 'Okay, if we could do it that fast, how do we do it?' And then it's just one bite of the apple at a time." Reframing the conversation toward solutions and problem solving helps eliminate the negatives. "You're always going to have little things that say no, but you have to keep trying to find a way to turn them into yeses."

"The electric school bus movement is happening really quick," Gil acknowledged. This movement is coming with significant funding. Federal programs, like EPA's $5 billion grant program, is just one opportunity. The IRA also offers tax credits, and states have funding opportunities as well, like the ones utilized by Gil at Stockton. "Well, the funding has never been better than right now, and I think it's the right idea, at the right time, right now."

In this work, Gil has had the opportunity to learn more about himself. He said, "I flourish well where you have to come up with ideas and be innovative, think outside the box, and don't take no for an answer." With the newness of the field, there are challenges, new requirements popping up, new grant opportunities, new partnerships that might make sense. People need to be thinking of solar, battery storage, electric buses, short-term and long-term greenhouse gas emissions. He described the challenge: "So you've got to spin 8 or 9 plates," and "all these plates are new concepts that people don't know about."

In his work, Gil keeps the future in sight. At some point, he knows mandates to make this transition will come. "I feel like if we wait until all the mandates happen, you're going to be pushed in line." Right now, he can work with different suppliers and be ahead of that curve. He recognized, "It's daunting for most people, but you have to find the champions in your district." He described it as looking out over a big highway that you must get across. It can feel overwhelming, but he advises taking it one step at a time to build the bridge to the other side.

- Find your champions.
- Talk to your utility provider.
- Find partners as the project engineers.
- Look to similar-sized districts that have done this work.
- Go after the money.

"All those people get you over . . . we've done it, at two different school districts in record time. It's possible." Even without making a full transition in Stockton, through relationships, resourcefulness, and persistence, Gil made significant advances. He was able to use the stories of smaller successes to lead to bigger ones. "There is no bad consequence from all these sustainability initiatives." He adds, "The benefits are worth it for our students and for our community."

REDUCING CARBON POLLUTION FROM SCHOOL FOOD

> I could see the amount of food waste that was being generated . . . from our schools. So that's when I started to say, "Look, we need to make some changes."
>
> —Janet Whited, San Diego Unified School District (SDUSD) in California

With 50 million students in public schools, the schools have many mouths to feed: they serve over 7 billion meals annually.[42] Food purchasing, menu choices, and decisions about food waste contribute to carbon pollution. Decisions around food in schools are an avenue for minimizing these emissions. Choosing to serve locally grown and sustainable food benefits both the environment and the local economy. Plus, local food vendors can help schools incorporate more fresh produce, which can be better for children's health. It is easier for schools to serve meals that use fresh local produce when they are equipped to support cooking from scratch rather than solely refrigerating and heating prepackaged food. A 2020 study from California found that cooking from scratch is occurring in many school districts and across district types (rural, urban, high-wealth, and low-wealth districts).[43] While cooking from scratch may be associated with higher labor costs, it is also associated with lower food cost, leaving researchers to find no significant difference in costs when school districts use cooking from scratch.[44]

As of 2020, thirty-four states and Washington, DC, had at least one policy, like farm-to-school programs, to promote locally sourced food in schools.[45] Eighteen states had policies to support the development of school gardens, which, when paired with food education, help students understand the benefits of healthy eating. In schools with school gardens and food education, researchers have found students eat more fruits and vegetables.[46] In Washington, DC, the district has a school garden program tied to teaching about food and environmental literacy, despite being in an urban community.[47] Rooftops, planters, and indoor grow towers can all help schools without extensive space.

Food waste is a pervasive challenge and a contributor to greenhouse gas emissions around the globe, and schools are no exception. Wasted food sitting in landfills emits methane, a greenhouse gas that is particularly good at trapping heat. Schools produce an estimated 530,000 tons of food waste annually.[48] In addition to being problematic for the environment, this wasted food also comes with a monetary cost. One study estimated the cost associated with food waste in schools nationally was $1.2 billion.[49]

Love Food, Not Waste: San Diego Unified School District

San Diego Unified School District (SDUSD) hired Janet Whited in 2009 as a recycling specialist. Her objective was to increase recycling across their campuses and save the district money. After being hired, she started traveling to the campuses to determine what sustainability efforts she could advance. One thing struck her as "pretty shocking" during her visits: the amount of food waste both from the students and from the kitchens. Janet remarked, "It became clear to me that was one of the components of the waste stream I needed to focus on." She understood that they needed an initiative to address this issue systemically. To do this she would have to work with the Food and Nutrition Services Department for the district.

Building the relationship with the Food and Nutrition Services Department took time, mainly because people felt overburdened already and they did not have time for additional work. They were focused on getting students fed. Getting them to engage required her to think carefully about their priorities. While waste might not be top priority on their agenda (feeding students was), cost was their second priority, and addressing waste could also help them address cost. Janet also found an ally in the Food Service Department: Fred Espinosa, manager of acquisition and production.

SDUSD serves about 120,000 students preK–12 across 226 educational facilities. About 60 percent of the district qualifies federally for free or reduced-price school meals, and free meals are available for all students. To serve meals, the district has twenty school production kitchens that each support about ten schools. To address the school district's issues with food waste, Janet, in partnership with Fred, created the Love Food Not Waste program. Adapting the EPA's food waste hierarchy, they created their own: feed the students was at the top, then came feed the budget (reduce purchasing), feed others (food recovery), feed the soil (compost), and feed the landfill.

After building the concept, they then needed to educate the community: the kitchen staff, custodial staff, students, educators, and more. Janet reflected that she has been pushed by Fred's motto, "Sell it, don't tell it." To build the buy-in required them to engage with staff members and hear their concerns, feedback, and input. Janet indicated they had to work to "change hearts and minds" in particular for the back-of-house kitchen staff. They had to understand how to reduce the amount of food they were preparing and learn how to forecast what would be eaten. Janet previously didn't know much about food service, but to work with other staff, she pushed herself to study the regulations they needed to follow and their general practices. Only through understanding their workflow and constraints would she be able to make recommendations for them and get over people's gut reaction, "I don't have time." For instance, it was a challenge to fulfill student food preferences within limited time frames: all students need to be offered the same food options regardless of whether they eat early or later in the day. So to be able to forecast preferences, they would need to keep that in mind and be "dialed in" to what kids will choose. They ended up implementing a few key strategies, including: (1) offering as opposed to automatically serving food and milk, (2) adding share tables where students can share unwanted food, and (3) reducing salad bar waste by changing the size of the insert pans. They worked to make the food look "tastefully empty," so that sparser amounts looked appetizing rather than overserving too much food in a deeper dish.

Their next priority on their list was "feeding others," also known as food recovery. Food recovery occurs when excess food from service can be saved and donated to others. Janet knew that when the last student in line had the same choices as the first, there was bound to be waste. Even if the goal is to have very little to donate, and even if you become better at purchasing the right amount of food, this is still a critical component of their program. They've worked to partner with hunger relief organizations (for example, the Salvation Army) to help feed others in the community. Leftovers are returned to the production kitchens and then picked up by the partner organizations.

Janet's concern was not initially related to climate change, but she recognized that connecting the food waste reduction initiative to climate change could help build additional buy-in locally. By tying the goal of reducing food waste to climate change, students started caring more, and this helped the initiative connect with broader city and community-wide climate change efforts. And not just students: Janet realized the food waste initiative has had the most success at different school sites when the entire community—from school leaders to kitchen staff, to custodial staff—care about making the initiative work.

The pandemic and staffing shortages and changes have posed challenges with the initiative. Food rescue had to be paused between 2020 through June 2022. But during the 2022–2023 school year, the school district was able to start again. Between 2016 and 2019, the Love Food Not

Waste program rescued 530,900 pounds of food waste, the equivalent of 422,300 meals, from the landfill. This work avoided the equivalent of 275,200 pounds of carbon dioxide being emitted to the atmosphere.[50]

Janet has advice to others embarking on this work: start with one priority and build the buy-in with food and nutrition services. She said, "dialing-in" on a goal—in this case, food waste—can really help with prioritization and building community support. With that starting point, a focused initiative can experience success and add additional priorities later, like food packaging.

CONCLUSION

Our carbon pollution with heat-trapping emissions has destabilized our climate. While we need to contend with the reality of a changing climate, we must also do what we can now to prevent the problem from getting worse by reducing our carbon pollution. Given the size and scope of the K–12 education sector, including buildings, energy use, transportation, and food, schools must be part of the solution. The United States can't decarbonize without schools. By harnessing the opportunity to decarbonize, school leaders can create healthy, sustainable learning environments where students can thrive.

Key Takeaways

1. Education leaders should consider the main sources of carbon pollution across buildings, energy, transportation, food, and waste.
2. Education leaders can identify strategic and equity-centered plans to reduce carbon pollution and collaborate with partners to help.
3. Education leaders can explain the multiple benefits to help build community buy-in, including the opportunity to save money on operations, create healthy learning environments for all students, and help students learn about climate solutions firsthand.

4. Education leaders can identify local, state, federal, and other funding opportunities, including through the Inflation Reduction Act and the Infrastructure Investment and Jobs Act, to offset costs associated with reducing carbon pollution.

6

The Power of Students and Collaboration

ON SEPTEMBER 6, 2022, *Shiva Rajbhandari, a high school senior in Boise, Idaho, sat nervously in his basement with family and friends watching the movie* Ferris Bueller's Day Off. *He was waiting for the news that with 56 percent of the vote, he had defeated an incumbent to win a seat on the Boise School Board just a week after his eighteenth birthday.*[1] *He recalled hearing the news in this setting as "humbling to be surrounded by all the people who made this possible."*[2]

In Boise, Shiva learned about climate change when he was in middle school, even though it was not included in the state standards, and he became concerned. This concern was made worse by the lack of action and attention from political leaders. He tried to do what he could on his own, like cutting down on his meat consumption, but he felt the urgency of the issue, and he craved more meaningful actions. In 2019, he joined a school strike on climate and felt increasingly motivated to act.

In 2020, two years prior to the school board election, Shiva had worked alongside other students with the Idaho Climate Justice League to push

Boise's school district to adopt a plan to transition to clean energy. They led a grassroots advocacy campaign with petitions, emails, and letters to encourage the school board to adopt a long-term sustainability plan. In doing this work, they sought to point out to the school board the opportunity for financial savings by reducing the costs associated with energy. At first, they did not hear much of a response from the school board, except for a stern conversation suggesting they not make demands of school board members. After eighteen months of organizing, the board passed a resolution called the Collective Commitment on Clean Energy. However, the resolution lacked time lines for implementation and highlighted work the district had already completed.[3]

This did not sit right with Shiva. In May 2022, Shiva started to consider what a school board run might entail, and after consulting with teachers, peers, and former board members, he made the decision to do it. He received support outside his community, and he was grateful that his message of climate action, mental health reform, and student voice resonated more broadly. Shiva's success made headlines, exemplifying the power of Gen Z activism to use not only protest and demonstrations to advocate for change but also their authority to earn a seat at the table. Shiva acknowledged, "Students belong in all places where decisions are made, but particularly where decisions are made on education."[4]

When I (Laura) first had the chance to work with Shiva, I told him how incredibly impressed I was by him and his decision to take action. He told me that this was not something special about him but that his empowerment came from years and years of his teachers encouraging him, helping him feel confident that he could make a difference. This is not about individual action but about people working together and supporting each other. Shiva recently reminded me, "Students are the people most familiar with what's going on in their schools and in their world. They have a vested interest in winning a livable future because they are going to see the full effects of the decisions adults are making today. They are powerful partners and capable leaders, and they deserve a seat at the table."

Shiva's experience highlights a critical point: individuals are doing incredible things, and we have highlighted many of them in this book, but these individuals cannot do it on their own. Shiva attributes much of his success to his experience in Boise Public Schools. He had educators who developed his understanding and helped him find his voice. When he decided to run for the school board, he had the support of his peers helping him shape his campaign and support from the community to push him across the finish line. Now, on the school board, Shiva recognizes the importance of working with other board members; administrators; educators; and, of course, students.

A changing climate is now the context in which our schools exist. It is an umbrella issue, meaning it impacts the learning, culture, operations, and budgets of our school systems. This also means that it impacts the people doing the work across the school system, from teachers and students to school bus drivers and school board members. To take action and help our school systems, education leaders must recognize the importance of collaboration, particularly with students. Without collaboration, the work across the school district will be disjointed. A school board might pass a resolution that never gets implemented, a sustainability director may have to be opportunistic rather than strategic, educators might feel vulnerable about pushing back without district support, or students may feel isolated in their concern and advocacy.

In this chapter, we outline how those connected to our education systems can advance collaborative action, including with students; we provide key questions to support effective collaboration; and we share stories of districts developing and implementing climate action plans across their districts. In each case, students, school board members, educators, and administration leaders have come together to advance solutions. Often the work started with organizing, followed by school board policy, cross-stakeholder planning, and implementation of comprehensive climate action plans. School systems are just at the beginning of understanding what it means to exist in a changing climate, and these climate action plans should be seen as dynamic. They can chart a course for action, and education stakeholders must continue to collaborate to remain flexible as our understandings and external contexts shift.

COLLABORATIVE CLIMATE ACTION PLANNING

Action on climate change is increasing rapidly across states, municipalities, and schools in the United States. Our school systems have the opportunity to learn from each other and from other efforts to chart comprehensive and systemic action in schools. For instance, for nearly two decades, cities around the globe have focused efforts on climate action planning. Climate action plans are intended to be strategic, systemic, and comprehensive guides for cities to mitigate their carbon pollution and adapt and build resilience to climate impacts. To develop these plans, city leaders bring various city-wide stakeholders together to collaborate.[5] In a 2023 report from This Is Planet Ed, we analyzed the climate action plans for the forty most populous cities to determine the extent to which they included schools in their strategy. Thirty-five of America's forty most populous cities had finalized climate action plans in place.[6] These plans outline comprehensive action for cities, but of those thirty-five, only twenty-three included a substantive strategy connected to K–12 school systems, and in many cases, those strategies were isolated to a particular program or topic.

School systems frequently operate under distinct governance models than cities and have tailored needs and opportunities, but school leaders can bring together a broad range of education stakeholders to develop local school district climate action plans. These climate action plans can create climate goals and targets for a district across climate education, adaptation, mitigation, and equity.

Establishing policies at the school board level can pave the way for collaboration. After advocacy from students across the district, Dallas Independent School District (IDS) passed an Environment and Climate Action

Resolution in 2020.[7] In that resolution, the board acknowledges, "In building the future through educating our youth, we recognize that we have a responsibility to be good stewards of the world that they will inherit, and that climate change threatens our ability to do that." The resolution goes on to emphasize what Dallas ISD will do: "The Dallas Independent School District Board of Trustees and the Superintendent of Schools shall relentlessly pursue systemic improvements to policies, programs, and practices in ways that enhance the District's sustainability initiatives to ensure that our youth inherit a healthy, clean, and vibrant world." To put this work in action, Dallas ISD established a committee to lead the effort that "shall be open to participation by board members, board appointees, administration, staff, parents, students, and community members, shall include the engagement of outside experts on environmental issues, and include representation from the City of Dallas." All these stakeholders have a role to play in advancing solutions, and all need a seat at the table. After passage of the resolution, school board member Ben Mackey noted, "It's the right thing to do. . . . Our mission in Dallas ISD is to educate all students to be able to go off and thrive in this world. Therefore, we have a parallel responsibility to give them a world to thrive in."[8]

ESTABLISHING COHERENCE

As school districts chart a path forward on climate action planning, leveraging lessons from other systemic improvement efforts can help set leaders up for success. For example, the Public Education Leadership Project (PELP) at Harvard Graduate School of Education developed the Coherence Framework to "help leaders recognize the interdependence of various aspects of their school district—its culture, systems and structures, resources, stakeholder relationships, and environment—and to understand how they reinforce one another."[9] Through the Coherence Framework, school leaders understand that climate change impacts the "environment" in which the school districts' context exists and how that sends ripples across all other components of educational work. Rather than allowing that disruption to occur, however, school leaders can further enhance the coherence across the district by advancing a systematic plan to address climate and advance solutions. The Coherence Framework considers how leaders can achieve coherence by:

- *Connecting the instructional core with a district-wide strategy for improvement*: The instructional core focuses on three key pillars: educators, students, and content. Climate both impacts and creates opportunities for engagement across the instructional core of schools' work. District-wide work on climate is an opportunity to strengthen the effectiveness of the instructional core.
- *Highlighting district elements that can support or hinder effective implementation*: School leaders should identify the needs, opportunities, and assets to support district-wide climate action, including the culture of the district.
- *Identifying interdependencies among district elements*: Because of the pervasive nature of climate, the number of existing interdependencies is vast. School leaders should assess the interdependencies within their own district to support comprehensive and coordinated action.
- *Recognizing forces in the environment that have an impact on the implementation of strategy*: Climate change is one of those factors directly affecting the school environment. Concerns about pushback from the external community may also impact district-wide action, but finding opportunities to build buy-in by emphasizing shared values can help. School leaders should also assess how policy opportunities, like the Inflation Reduction Act (IRA), can accelerate and provide resources for district-level work.

Advancing climate solutions requires us to act collaboratively, plan strategically, and communicate effectively to ensure lasting change. Policies, collaborative planning, and effective implementation of the plan can create the conditions for systemic action and success. To shift mind-sets toward collaboration on climate, school leaders should consider the following questions.

Climate Collaboration Questions

- Who are the stakeholders in my school district? What are their pressing priorities and concerns? How can we meaningfully engage students, particularly students from historically marginalized communities, in district-wide action?
- How can we establish a process for collaborative climate action planning in our school district?
- How does district-wide climate action align with our district's mission and values? What are the shared values of the broader community? How can action on climate change connect to our community's shared values?
- What are the barriers to district-wide implementation? How can those barriers be removed?

Climate Collaboration Mind-Set

To have a climate collaboration mind-set, school leaders, administrators, and educators should:

- Understand the roles and responsibilities of different stakeholders across the school district.
- Create opportunities for students to participate meaningfully in district planning and action.
- Develop a process to engage in systemic and comprehensive climate action planning.
- Determine how to align climate action with the school district's mission and shared values.
- Commit time to building buy-in from stakeholders across the school district and community.
- Consider and remove barriers to collaboration and partnerships.

Collaboration across stakeholders, schools, and roles and responsibilities in school systems is no easy task. People come with their unique perspectives, and working in silos may seem easier, but working in silos will only exacerbate the challenges we face. People who work in education generally come to this work with a common desire to provide better opportunities for children and young people. As we will see later in this chapter, to provide better opportunities for young people at this moment, we need to face the challenges of a changing climate and advance solutions across our school systems together. And school districts across the country are demonstrating how this can be accomplished.

STARTING WITH STUDENTS

> I learned a lot about how local level change takes place and a lot of that comes with . . . persistence.
>
> —Andie Madsen, former student at West High School in Salt Lake City, Utah

Students are the primary constituents in schools, and young people have the most at stake with our changing climate given the increasing impacts in the decades to come. Students can be key leaders and key collaborators as schools take action on climate change. But education leaders need to create space and opportunities for students to be successful. This means recognizing that including student voices in decision making adds value to the conversation. It means ensuring that student engagement is not an add-on or performative but embedded in the process. It means recognizing the barriers to student participation in conversation and proactively taking steps to reduce those barriers. And it means shifting the assumptions of students as activists and agitators to allies and partners. Performative actions, like inviting students to a meeting without engaging them in dialogue or decision making or allowing barriers to remain in place, devalues student perspectives and prevents them from meaningful participation.

Education leaders should be purposeful in creating the space for students to learn. For instance, at the beginning of a meeting, education leaders can state the intent of collaboration and valuing the perspectives of everyone in the room. This helps create a space where people feel appreciated and thus are more willing to ask questions and take risks. We rely too often on acronyms or jargon in education. This can inadvertently create a power imbalance. Avoiding these terms or creating glossaries so all understand what they mean can help make the conversation more accessible. Education leaders also shouldn't assume that students understand the processes we've grown accustomed to as adults, like agendas or budgets. Ensuring that students have the information that they need in advance of collaborative meetings can help students feel more prepared.

When education leaders engage students in the process of systemic climate action, they impart key lessons that students will benefit from in the long term. Students learn the importance of civic participation and also develop interpersonal, leadership, and communication skills. When students are involved in systemic climate action in partnership with adults, their climate anxiety feelings may be reduced, and they can develop agency to advance solutions.

Students as Leaders: Salt Lake City School District

As a tenth-grader at West High School in Salt Lake City, Andie Madsen joined her high school environmental club. Salt Lake City School District enrolls about twenty thousand students, with about 53 percent of the students coming from low-income families.[10] The school district includes twenty-eight elementary schools, six middle schools, and three high schools.[11] Andie acknowledged, "Growing up there [Utah], I just have this intense connection to the landscape and the outdoors." Prior to joining the club, Andie had not been aware of the changes to the climate around her. Through the club and her activism, the changes became more apparent: the poorer air quality in Salt Lake City; the less reliable snowpack; and the threats to their city's namesake, the drying up of the Great Salt Lake.[12] Andie said that her activism started on a "career high." The environmental club worked with Utah Youth Environmental Solutions (UYES), a student-led organization that actively pushed the state legislature to pass a bill acknowledging the realities of climate change.[13] When that resolution passed, Andie said she was "hooked." Inspired by the collective effort to have a conservative state acknowledge climate change, Andie sought additional opportunities to push for change, and her school district offered her an opportunity to do just that.

In her tenth-grade year at East High School, Mahider Tadesse took an environmental science class where she learned about climate issues. She saw climate as "something that we need to act on quickly." Learning about intersectionality and climate change motivated Mahider to act. "I wasn't just tackling an environmental issue, but also a social issue." But she didn't know where to start. In the next year, Mahider decided to start an environmental club at East High School. The club's initial efforts were small in scale, like starting a community garden, but then they heard the news that students from West High School were advocating for a school board resolution. Mahider recognized this as an opportunity to advance "ideas for sustainability beyond just the school level and expand to the district level."

When students from West High School and East High School came together initially to push the school board to adopt a resolution, the students felt unheard by their representatives. Mahider described this as the school board's "skepticism with a fully student-led resolution." Andie felt as though they "were patted on the back and spoken for," which she described as "insulting." According to Andie, the students wanted to "work with them [the school board] on an equal, collaborative, and communal basis."

Both Andie and Mahider realized that they had to prove they could be taken seriously by the school board. They worked hard with their peers to figure out the school board's pressing concerns and reframe their arguments to address those concerns. Mahider noted, "It wasn't a linear process." Specifically, the students were pushed to address the economics of the resolution: How would the district pay for this? How would this resolution be financially beneficial? And they needed to demonstrate that there was sufficient community support. Mahider acknowledged they needed to be "convincing and persuasive."

The students worked to bring in renewable energy specialists to explain to the school board how the resolution would be implemented. They brought in letters and testimony from the broader community, including educators, school staff, and parents. They had the support of the district sustainability director, and they proved to the school board that enacting their resolution was not a huge financial risk. Andie said, "Once we were persistent and able to show the legitimacy of what we were asking for and all the community support . . . we were able to be on equal footing with the representatives, and that's when real progress got to be made."

In June 2020, the school board unanimously passed a resolution "to establish goals for sustainability, clean energy, and carbon neutrality."[14] The resolution acknowledges the damaging effects of climate change and establishes the board's commitment to "making positive, tangible changes to mitigate climate change, and to ensure that every effort is made to conserve energy and natural resources while exercising sound financial management." The resolution established the district-wide goal of using 100 percent clean renewable energy by 2030 and achieving carbon neutrality in all district operations by 2040. The resolution also put in place a task force to implement the resolution that consisted of "community members, students, energy experts, partners, and district staff, and will be chaired by the executive director of auxiliary services."

Mahider served as one of the student members on the task force, which developed and released the district's sustainability action plan in September 2021.[15] Since the action plan release, the school district has entered into a $29.5 million guaranteed energy savings performance contract to support its transition to clean energy.[16] Through this agreement, the district will pay the loan back with the amount of money they save from what would have otherwise gone to energy costs. Through the contract, the school district is installing solar panels, adjusting lighting, increasing efficient water use, and supporting building electrification. They anticipate that this work will save the district $1.3 million annually. Andie recognized that even though this effort started with students, she appreciates "the district matching the enthusiasm."

Mahider offers advice to others embarking on their own efforts to push schools to take action: "It's important to not be afraid of not being as credible or not being as qualified to be in these spaces. Because, although it is helpful to have the formal education behind sustainability . . . those personal narratives are also very important."

WORKING ACROSS SILOS

> To achieve transformative impact, PGCPS [Prince George's County Public Schools] cannot go it alone. We must collaborate with the Maryland State Department of Education (MSDE), County leadership, PGCPS students, parents and staff, PGCPS alumni, advocacy groups and local organizations in partnership towards systemic change. Only together can we work to envision, plan, and build an inclusive, prosperous, and resilient future.
>
> —Prince George's County Public Schools,
> Climate Change Action Plan

Our school systems are not set up for collaboration. The legacy of egg-crate classrooms, the problem with educational reforms going in and out of fashion, the layers of stakeholders, and the bureaucratic structures of school systems can create barriers to collaboration. School systems, particularly larger school systems, have various departments tasked with specific areas of focus. Operations and academics do not often connect across issues. To advance climate action and support student learning about solutions, however, operations and academics must work together. School leaders can demonstrate their commitment to work collaboratively on these issues in the policies they establish as well as the way they staff the implementation in the district. We saw how the Dallas school board highlighted both academics and operations in their resolution and how students in Salt Lake City worked with the school board to implement change. Students took similar collaborative action in Denver Public Schools (DPS).

In April 2022, students succeeded in pushing the DPS school board to establish policies to include climate goals in the district's long-term vision and strategy. The district then embarked on an eighteen-month planning process, which included a greenhouse gas inventory, stakeholder engagement, and a financial assessment. Three North Star goals guide the DPS plan: environmental protection; economic prosperity; and social development.[17] The plan calls for action across the built environment, transportation, resource management, wellness, engagement and environmental justice, and career and curriculum. The district also created a data dashboard to communicate their goals and monitor their progress.

LeeAnn Kittle started at DPS in 2020 as a director of sustainability, and she worked with the students through their advocacy efforts with the school board. Now, LeeAnn works on implementation of the climate action plan across different departments in the district. In an *Education Week* profile, LeeAnn noted, "I know how to really engage folks because no matter where they are on the topic, they're going to relate to finances, the environment, or enhancing our community."[18] In 2023, after years as the director of sustainability within the operation's offices, LeeAnn's role shifted: she became the district's first executive director for sustainability. This new position elevated the role of climate action to the superintendent's leadership team rather than keeping it housed in operations, which demonstrated school leadership commitment. It allows her to collaborate more easily across the district's schools, both on operations and the academic side. With decisions like shifting LeeAnn's role from operations to the superintendent's office, school leaders communicated their prioritization of climate action and helped to reduce barriers to implementation.

The possibilities for collaboration extend beyond the school systems themselves into the broader community. Many cities, municipalities, and states have or are developing climate action plans. Our school systems can be critical partners in those efforts, and cities, municipalities, and states can be essential partners for schools to inform and help guide the work.

Partnering Across Many Stakeholders: PGCPS

On July 20, 1977, Johnstown, Pennsylvania, had almost twelve inches of rain over the course of several hours.[19] Dams failed, eighty-four people lost their lives, and the downtown area was devastated. Pamela Boozer-Strother was eight years old at the time of the flood and felt privileged to live on a hill. Her father had to go downtown, and her mother, crying, took her to look at the town from above. Witnessing the destruction from extreme weather, Pamela acknowledged that she would "never forget the trauma of it . . . that severe weather event experience just doesn't leave you."

Decades later, after receiving her MBA, Pamela grew increasingly concerned with the maintenance she was seeing in Maryland's public schools. Maryland's aging school infrastructure resulted in wasted money and inefficiencies, and the legislature couldn't figure out a solution to address it. They talked initially about paying people less, and Pamela's gut told her, "That's not going to work." She wanted to help address the issue, and she won a seat on the Prince George's County school board in 2018.

PGCPS in Maryland is among the largest school districts in the country, serving over 130,000 students across two hundred schools.[20] About 60 percent of the students are from low-income families, and the size of the district means that students come from urban, suburban, and rural communities. The district's mission is to "provide a transformative educational experience anchored by excellence in equity—developing 21st century competencies and enabling each student's unique brilliance to flourish in order to build empowered communities and a more inclusive and just world."[21]

Once she was on the school board, parents approached Pamela about advocating for climate friendly food and clean energy school buildings. She toured schools in her district that had been forced to cancel recess due to flooding. She also took notice of extreme weather events around the world. As the memories of her personal experience with the Johnstown, Pennsylvania, flood guided her, Pamela increasingly realized the damaging impacts of our reliance on fossil fuels. She noted, "When I started seeing the world that our children are inheriting, I began to have thoughts about my son."

Pamela's growing awareness coincided with hearing concerns from other parents across the county. Another parent and leader of the local Sierra Club Climate Parents chapter, Joseph Jakuta, along with students from Eleanor Roosevelt High School, presented at a board meeting on the need for sustainable school infrastructure. The Volkswagen (VW) Environmental Mitigation Trust, which was established after the automaker submitted misleading federal emissions tests, created funding opportunities to reduce pollution from transportation, including school transportation. At Chispa Maryland, a Latino parent led a Clean Rides for Kids campaign and presented on electric school buses, including advocating for the Volkswagen settlement to be used by the school district to purchase electric school buses. As Pamela reflected, "They came independently but the message was clear." She knew the board of education needed to pursue a more comprehensive effort that involved disparate members of the community.

To develop a comprehensive plan and goals for the district, the Prince George's County Board of Education established the Climate Change Action Plan (CCAP) Focus Work Group in March 2021 thanks to Pamela's and Joseph's leadership. The work group brought together leaders from across the community, including students; parents; educators; staff members; school board members; county council members; state legislators; and experts in design, food, energy, transportation, and equity. To develop their plan, they learned from members of the community. They held panels to hear from environmental justice advocates, labor leaders, elected officials, curriculum experts, and students. The work group established four guiding principles:

1. We believe in broad Work Group member buy-in.
2. We believe in science.
3. We believe in transparency, equity, and inclusivity.
4. We believe in accountability.[22]

Pamela had anticipated more challenges in building community buy-in than they actually received. She highlighted a quote in the action plan from Dr. Alvin Thornton, former chair of the PGCPS Board of Education: "Climate action is about equity. It is the next broad paradigm that the people of Prince George's County can come together in oneness to benefit our children. All children should have equal access to a healthy environment. It is a fundamental right." Grounding their effort in their responsibility to the next generation brought people together. They also took the process of the work group seriously, "It was a rigorous commitment . . . everyone on that group was a professional. None of them were going to give up their time if we were not operating at a very high level of professionalism."

The board of education approved the working group's CCAP on April 28, 2022. The plan focused on eight commitments:

1. Support environmental justice through climate curriculum, training, and partnerships.
2. Reduce carbon footprint from PGCPS buildings.
3. Commit to renewable energy sources for a net-zero emissions future.
4. Commit to low-carbon school transportation.

5. Reduce food waste and grow climate-friendly food.
6. Commit to sustainable materials management and procurement.
7. Commit to climate-resilient land management.
8. Lead by example to support transformational change.

Getting the plan developed and approved was an essential springboard for action. Pamela acknowledged that that was just a first step: "Don't rest and think [we've got] this solved because we have a document and policies." She added, "It's now on us to do the work." With this plan in place, they created professional learning opportunities for educators and field experience programs for students, added solar panels to schools, acquired electric school buses, and conducted energy audits. The commitment to grow and serve climate-friendly foods seemed the most challenging for Pamela because of the loss of farmland and a lack of infrastructure to support cooking from scratch in schools across the state.

Even with potential implementation challenges ahead, climate action has presented unique opportunities for partnership, particularly with municipalities and elected officials. The state, county, and school system were all trying to advance action simultaneously, which Pamela found helpful. The school district could tell the elected officials: "Go ahead and vote . . . because we'll be ready." If they passed a climate bill, the school district was ready to take advantage of it. Municipalities within the school district have also stepped up to fund climate action in schools for things like stormwater management or outdoor learning projects. Pamela reflected on the work across her communities, the school system, and the state, "Climate action is connecting us."

CONCLUSION

Despite many competing demands, school districts across the country are taking action on climate change by developing and implementing comprehensive climate action plans. These plans help draw on the needs and assets of the district and connect to the broader mission, vision, and instructional core. To develop these climate action plans, school districts must emphasize the role of collaboration across stakeholders. Students are key constituents of the education sector and have the most at stake with issues of climate change; thus, they should be at the center of district-wide action. To partner with young people meaningfully, ensuring sufficient support throughout the process can help make climate action an active learning experience for students. Collaborative climate action planning that includes students is a critical step for action across our K–12 schools and for helping all students to thrive.

Key Takeaways

1. Students, educators, parents or caregivers, staff, administrators, and education leaders all have relevant experiences, expertise, and concerns about climate change, and all have a right to engage with systemic solutions.
2. Climate change action plans can be used to support collaborative and comprehensive action across teaching and learning, mitigation, adaptation, and equity.
3. Including all stakeholders—and students—to participate authentically in climate change action planning can help ensure community buy-in and broader commitment to effective implementation.
4. To include students meaningfully, school leaders must remove barriers to student participation and value students' perspectives in decision making.

7

Leading Change and Taking Action

"Maybe" is not a cautious word. It is a defiant claim of possibility in the face of a status quo we are unwilling to accept.

—Eric Young, founder of the Social Projects Studio, Toronto, Canada

IN PREVIOUS CHAPTERS, we have followed the journeys of students, educators, and others who chose to take action on climate change in their schools and communities. We haven't told their stories because these people are superheroes with rare gifts and talents. Our goal isn't to celebrate their unique abilities or put them on a pedestal. Few of them saw themselves as climate leaders. They are just folks like the rest of us. But along their paths, they were inspired and compelled to respond to factors like extreme weather events, their own growing awareness of the scientific consensus about climate change, and/or the demands of young people in their lives. Their stories and the ideas we have related through their stories are adaptable to schools and communities throughout the country. The message here is this: you can do it, too.

The approach you take will depend on your unique context and community. For Jonathan, the journey started when he began asking the education leaders in his network, including school board members, district leaders, nonprofit leaders, teachers, and principals, about how climate change impacted their priorities. Those early conversations built his knowledge about the state of the field and sparked ideas about what might be needed to catalyze action. For Laura, it was reckoning with the science of the Intergovernmental Panel on Climate Change (IPCC) reports, the implications for her own children, and a decision to put her education policy background and skills to new uses at this intersection of climate and education.

As you step into a role as a leader on climate, remember that you won't be alone. In our experience, the networks of practitioners and advocates working on climate action in schools are as generous and collaborative as they are smart and determined. We are still in the early stages of mobilizing America's public schools to address climate change, which means you will probably find yourself mingling with others at the forefront of the movement before too long. Rather than being intimidated, know that others will be learning and trying out ideas alongside you. Don't hesitate to seek help or reach out with an email or a direct message—even if you haven't met before. Some of our own most fruitful contacts and collaborations have begun that way.

In this chapter, we turn to your role in and opportunities for taking climate action in your school and community. Our intention here is to distill the concepts of mitigation, adaptation, and education into practical frameworks that you can use to implement change in K–12 schools. The chapter concludes with our fellow practitioners' perspectives, guiding ideas, and high-level mind-sets to consider as you lead change in your educational institution and community.

WHAT NEEDS TO CHANGE

School District Commitments for Climate Change Education, Adaptation, and Mitigation

In previous chapters, we delved into education (how the curricula and experiences schools provide students must adjust to prepare them for our changing world), adaptation (how schools need to adjust given the changing climate), and mitigation (how schools can reduce their impact on the climate). Here, we ask: How do these concepts apply to the various structures and responsibilities of a school district? Through our work at UndauntedK12 and This Is Planet Ed, we have identified areas where district leaders can take action to ensure that their schools manifest sustainability, resilience, and relevant education given the changing climate. As a result of these actions, schools will be equipped to provide students with the tools and experiences they need to create a resilient, equitable, and sustainable future. Recognizing that climate change is a threat multiplier that amplifies existing patterns of injustice within society, school districts must bring an equity and justice focus to making decisions and allocating resources throughout these priorities.

Education

Empowering school systems engage, prepare, and support students in a changing climate by incorporating:

- *Essential climate concepts*: Ensure that every student has opportunities to understand essential climate concepts: Earth is our home. It's getting hotter because of us. It's changing now, and it's impacting us. But together, we can make the changes we need for a brighter future.
- *Cross-curricular learning*: Apply a climate lens across grades and subjects to enable students to understand the causes, consequences, and solutions to climate change holistically. Seek opportunities to

integrate learning about climate throughout existing lessons, curricula, and activities, and ensure that educators feel supported and prepared to teach climate across the curriculum.

- *Clean economy career pathways*: Expose students to clean economy career pathways and integrate sustainability across career and technical education.
- *Social-emotional support*: Recognize that the changing climate and extreme weather have an impact on the well-being of children and adults in schools, and provide support to process experiences and fears, build resilience, and participate in shaping solutions.
- *Extracurricular learning*: Collaborate with partners across the community to support informal learning opportunities and extracurricular activities to engage students in deeper learning and solutions given the changing climate.

Adaptation

Resilient school systems adapt to the changing climate by incorporating:

- *Climate risk assessments*: Assess vulnerabilities and risks posed by climate change by considering factors such as the likelihood and severity of events, for example, extreme heat, floods, hurricanes, wildfires, and other climate-related hazards; geographic location; vulnerability of infrastructure; disruptions to transportation, utilities, and access to essential services; and community demographics.
- *Climate adaptation planning*: Develop and implement plans by involving school administrators, teachers, students, parents, local government officials, and community organizations to proactively address identified risks and enhance capacity to withstand and recover from climate-related impacts. Plans may include infrastructure upgrades, development of emergency response protocols, integration of climate-resilient curriculum, partnerships with local emergency management agencies, and provision of training and capacity-building activities for staff and students.

- *Healthy environments*: Provide climate-resilient learning environments that promote student health and well-being and are conducive to their engagement and learning, for example, shaded schoolyards and indoor learning spaces with modern technologies to maintain indoor air quality (IAQ) and thermally comfortable classrooms.
- *Sustainable school grounds*: Reduce the total area of school grounds that is paved or otherwise impermeable, and increase the area planted with sustainable, preferably native ground cover. Shade playgrounds and other areas where students play, congregate, and learn with trees or other sustainable cover to reduce heat impacts and improve water retention.
- *Emergency preparation*: Ensure that schools are ready to protect and support student learning and well-being (including social-emotional learning and mental health) through extreme weather and other climate-driven crises, as well as other types of emergencies, and to serve as centers of community resilience.

Mitigation

Sustainable school systems mitigate their carbon pollution by incorporating:

- *Clean renewable power*: Increase reliance on power produced from clean renewable sources—including, to the extent possible, electricity generated by equipment installed on district property—with the goal of eventually powering district operations exclusively with electricity from zero-emission renewables.
- *Electric equipment*: Install modern electric equipment—including heating, ventilation, and air-conditioning (HVAC) systems, water heaters, and cooking equipment—as part of any new construction or renovation. Identify opportunities to replace all legacy fossil-fuel-dependent equipment within the life cycle of such equipment.
- *Zero-emission vehicles*: Select zero-emission vehicles for purchase or lease whenever a suitable vehicle exists for a district need and

wherever necessary infrastructure (e.g., electric vehicle charging stations) is accessible, with the goal of transitioning the entire district vehicle fleet to zero-emission vehicles.

- *Sustainable food*: Increase the portion of produce used by district food services that is fresh, locally sourced, minimally processed or packaged, and prepared on-site. Decrease waste through education and by composting food and food waste.

These commitments hold implications for various departments on your district's organizational chart, including transportation, buildings and grounds, curriculum and instruction, and food services. In districts that have embarked on comprehensive climate change action plans, such as Prince George's County Public Schools (PGCPS) in Maryland and Denver Public Schools (DPS), leaders across these and other departments collaborate to achieve district-wide goals. The process of change can also start within a single department. Think of Gil Rosas (see chapter 5), who started deploying electric school buses and charging infrastructure in Stockton, California. Now he's director of sustainability in Modesto, replicating his success with transportation and pursuing district-wide sustainability initiatives.

Our responsibility to students and to a livable future demands that we pursue commitment and action in each of the three areas (education, adaptation, and mitigation). You will know based on your role and context where you are best positioned to lead and contribute.

TAP INTO YOUR POWER

Opportunities Abound to Drive Action Whatever Your Role or Context

As we have shared throughout the preceding chapters, stakeholders across school districts can all contribute to solutions and help accelerate systemic action. Although far from exhaustive, the list below outlines the strengths of various stakeholders (listed alphabetically) and their opportunities to lead.

District Operations and Sustainability Staff

Administrative staff members and sustainability directors can collaborate with school board members and superintendents to develop and implement policies that promote sustainability and climate resilience across all aspects of school operations. They collect and analyze data related to energy consumption, waste generation, transportation, food systems, student access to climate education, and other relevant metrics to identify opportunities for improvement and track progress toward sustainability goals. They support the integration of climate education into the curriculum by partnering with educators to turn school campuses into learning labs about sustainability and resilience.

Educators

Educators can develop curriculum materials and engage students in lessons that incorporate and bring a climate lens to their teaching. They can facilitate hands-on learning experiences, such as outdoor field trips, environmental projects, and gardening activities, to deepen students' understanding of climate issues and foster a sense of connection to the natural world. Educators can empower students to take action on climate change by providing opportunities for advocacy, leadership, and civic engagement both inside and outside the classroom.

Parents and Caregivers

Parents and caregivers can support climate initiatives in schools by participating in parent-teacher associations, attending school board meetings, and advocating for climate-conscious policies and practices. They can reinforce environmental values and principles at home by modeling sustainable behaviors, discussing climate issues with their children, and supporting their involvement in eco-friendly activities and initiatives.

Principals

Principals can use their leadership to emphasize the alignment of climate action with their core school mission and culture. School leaders can set the tone for environmental responsibility on their campuses by promoting sustainable practices such as energy conservation, sustainable transportation options, waste reduction, and recycling. They can work with educators to integrate climate education across various subjects and grade levels, ensuring that students develop the knowledge, skills, and attitudes needed to address climate challenges. Principals can engage with parents, local businesses, and community organizations to garner support for sustainability initiatives and create opportunities for collaboration and collective action.

School Board Members

As key policy makers, school board members can leverage their essential role in prioritization, budgeting, and superintendent hiring and evaluation to support climate action in schools. School board members can help create the conditions for climate action success within school communities. Collaborating with district staff members can help ensure effective implementation of any policies, and partnering with students and parents can help build buy-in and ensure that climate action is relevant to the primary constituents in schools.

School Support Staff

Support staff such as custodians, maintenance workers, food service personnel, and transportation personnel can contribute to climate solutions by implementing energy-saving measures, reducing waste, and promoting sustainable practices in their respective roles. They can serve as ambassadors for sustainability within the school community; raise awareness about climate issues; and encourage participation in climate action initiatives among students, parents, and colleagues.

Students

Students can take on leadership roles in advocating for climate action within their schools and communities, organizing initiatives, and campaigning to raise awareness and promote sustainable practices. They can actively participate in sustainability projects and initiatives on campus; contribute ideas, solutions, and efforts to reduce a school's carbon pollution; and enhance resilience to climate change. Students can also collaborate with educators, school leaders, and community stakeholders to cocreate learning opportunities, projects, and events that empower peers and inspire collective action on climate issues.

Superintendents

Superintendents can play a crucial role in setting the tone and vision for climate action within a school district. They can champion sustainability initiatives, allocate financial resources for climate-related programs and infrastructure upgrades, and provide professional learning opportunities for staff to integrate climate education into the curriculum. Superintendents can also forge partnerships with local government agencies, community organizations, and businesses to access additional resources, expertise, and funding opportunities for climate initiatives.

PRACTICAL STEPS TO TAKE ACTION

Starting to Lead from Wherever You Are in Your District and Community

> Never doubt that a small group of thoughtful, committed citizens can change the world; indeed, it's the only thing that ever has.
>
> —Margaret Mead[1]

The process of social or organizational change is rarely linear and seldom follows a predefined path. In each situation, individual, idiosyncratic people come together to create change. So your action steps and your district's path will be your own. With that in mind, we offer this framework to approach the big questions and considerations as you navigate and support your district to develop a comprehensive climate change action plan.

Step 1. Find Allies and Partners

Regardless of your role within the community, we promise you are not alone in your desire to prioritize climate action in your schools. As the stories in previous chapters illustrate, you can find allies throughout your community: parents concerned about their children riding diesel buses, student athletes affected by extreme weather-related cancellations, local business leaders invested in the clean energy transition, local farmers dealing with disruption and crop damage due to extreme weather. Seek out these allies, and notice others—among students, teachers, parents, district administrators, community members, board members—who share your passion for addressing climate change. Not everyone will be or even needs to be as committed to addressing climate change as you are. Start discussions, and you'll discover collaborators, allies, and coconspirators who can help you make a difference in your school or district.

In our experience, people are drawn to climate action for two main reasons: their connections to others and their connections to their environment or local community. As you build your team of allies within the community, remember that people stay engaged—even through inevitable obstacles and setbacks—when they feel a sense of belonging in the group. Sharing your own climate awakening story and how you see the impacts of climate change on your community will nurture a personal connection that motivates those you engage. It's important to connect the dots between your school's experiences with cancellations of school or sporting events from extreme heat and increased cases of asthma and school absences from wildfire smoke, and damage and degradation of buildings at your school and in your community from extreme storms. Build your understanding of how extreme weather is affecting your community, and point others toward the best resources you can find for data on climate changes and impacts in your region.

One-on-one meetings are an important way to connect with potential allies. In just twenty to thirty minutes, you can learn valuable information and insights into their interests, beliefs, and connections to climate action. You will deepen relationships and build shared purpose as you invite those you engage to share their own climate stories and prompt them to reflect on how climate change affects them personally. Always conclude these meetings with a next step, such as an invitation to another conversation, meeting, or activity.

Across the country, climate action is happening in politically "red" (conservative), "blue" (liberal), and "purple" (mixed) communities, and the most effective messaging and approach may differ for each. For example, a school district in a conservative community might have an energy manager, while a district in a more liberal place might call a role with a similar job description a sustainability manager. Independent of local politics, we find that schools that invest in energy-efficient, cost-effective technologies are generally well received because all communities expect their public school districts to use taxpayer dollars responsibly. To bridge any potential divides, it is helpful to start conversations with shared values and language.

Step 2. Assess District Needs and Opportunities

Once you have a friend or two to work with, it is helpful to have a baseline understanding of the starting point for your district, who to engage, and your district's most pressing needs and potential assets. Make a list of what you know and what you want to learn about the current status of climate action and sustainability activities within your school or district. This information will be critical in forming a plan of action. Below are some questions you might consider to start mapping the work in your school district.

- *Collaborators*: To get things started, who most needs to be brought into the climate change conversation? Consider the stakeholders across your community, including students, and identify key stakeholders to engage in conversation. It is especially critical to ensure that you engage diverse collaborators and conversation partners, including those most impacted by climate change and environmental injustice.

- *Motivation*: What is the district's mission? Why might different leaders in your school and community feel inspired to act? What matters most to them? In relation to climate, what values or concerns might you all share? Understanding leaders' motivation is important to connecting action on climate to core district priorities rather than positioning it as "another thing" or a siloed priority for district leaders.
- *Education*: What are the existing needs and assets as they relate to supporting teaching and learning on climate change, climate solutions, and sustainability across the curriculum? How are existing career and technical education programs preparing students for the clean, green, and changing local economy? Educators prepare young people for the future, and educators need support aligning teaching and learning to our changing climate context.
- *Adaptation*: What are the likely climate risks for your school district? What are the existing needs and assets as they relate to supporting the district in facing climate-related learning disruption? With proactive planning and preparation, districts will be better prepared to respond to and navigate the uncertainty and challenges ahead.
- *Mitigation*: What are the existing needs and assets as they relate to the district's infrastructure, energy, transportation, and food use? Does your district have an existing sustainability plan? Look for opportunities that both decrease the district's contributions to greenhouse gas emissions and have a positive impact on the bottom line.
- *Equity*: How are students, families, and schools differentially impacted by climate change within the district? Identifying the differential impacts of climate change on students, families, and schools in your community can help you build a plan that seeks to advance equity and create a more sustainable and resilient school system for all students.

Step 3. Get Organized and Choose a Target

Depending on your role within the school district, you may have different paths for advocacy and leadership. The focus of your advocacy and leadership will also depend on your community and district context. It will be helpful to develop a clear goal for what you are trying to achieve in your school district based on the needs, opportunities, and assets in your community.

There are opportunities to win on this issue every school year. For instance, if your school or district is upgrading an HVAC system or replacing school kitchen equipment, you can work to ensure installation of modern all-electric machines and systems. If your district is hiring a new facilities director, you can work to ensure that they are committed to sustainability and climate action as part of the hiring criteria. If your district is investing in school infrastructure, you can work to build awareness of the new federal incentives and grant opportunities available to help schools deploy clean energy technologies. You can advocate for a school board and district-wide commitment to develop and implement a comprehensive climate change action plan. Here are some questions to consider:

- What do you want to see change? Will you ask your district to make commitments related to mitigation, adaptation, and education? Will you focus on two to three areas where you see the most opportunity for quick wins and impact? Will you push for accountability to make progress and fulfill existing commitments?
- Do you already have positional or formal authority (district administrator, school board member, principal, etc.) to change how your school or district operates? Or are you a student or parent who will need to influence those with formal authority over policy, budgets, and purchasing decisions?
- Do you need a school board resolution or policy to accelerate the change?

Step 4. Pursue a Comprehensive Plan, Seize Moments for Action, and Keep Learning Along the Way

Every community needs to develop and implement comprehensive K–12 climate change action plans that consider their district's needs and opportunities to mitigate, adapt, educate, and advance equity. Regardless of where your district is on that planning journey or of your role in education, moments of opportunity arise nearly every day where your leadership and climate lens on decision making can make a difference.

Pursuing a District-Wide Climate Change Action Plan You will ideally be in a position to work collaboratively across your district to develop a comprehensive climate change action plan with goals for mitigation, adaptation, education, and equity. A school board resolution or policy is generally helpful to kick-start the planning process for the climate change action plan. The school board resolution can establish why this work matters to your district and create a working group with various stakeholders (ideally those collaborators previously identified) to engage in the planning process.

The working group can leverage the baseline information you have gathered on the needs and assets within the district and collect additional research to inform planning. Within the climate change action plan, the working group should define measurable objectives and targets within each major goal area and work to identify the resources and supports that the district will need to execute the plan effectively. The school district climate change action plan should also address the when and how by establishing timelines and specifying strategies and tactics.

You don't have to create everything from scratch. You can find artifacts from the convening, planning, and implementation process of the PGCPS climate change working group on the district website. There, you will find meeting agendas, videos of meeting discussions, participant lists, and progress reports.[2] The UndauntedK12 website also features model resolutions and action plans from leading districts around the country to use as templates or to adapt.

Finding Moments for Action Developing a comprehensive, district-wide climate change action plan requires extensive collaboration spanning months among district departments and community partners. It's also vital to engage opportunistically and seize moments for immediate action and to ensure that every decision incorporates a climate lens to drive meaningful change. Let Margaret Mead's words from the start of this section be your guide: you can act with confidence and remember that the individuals and small groups of people who show up to engage and participate often have tremendous influence on decisions.

Here are some key moments when leaders and advocates might bring a climate lens and questions into deliberations about the core functions and governance of the school district:

- *Establishing district goals and priorities*: When your district is establishing district-wide goals and priorities, you can work to incorporate climate action. For instance, you can look for an opportunity to incorporate any of the climate education, adaptation, and mitigation commitments (introduced earlier in this chapter) within the broader district goals.
- *Reviewing or updating existing district plans and policies*: When your district is reviewing existing plans or policies, you can make sure these revisions include a climate lens.
- *Hiring superintendents and other senior staff*: When your district is hiring a superintendent or other senior leader, you can make sure candidates are asked about their knowledge of climate change issues; their understanding of the impacts of extreme weather on student health and learning; and how they would prioritize addressing mitigation, adaptation, and education—all with equity at the center.
- *Setting and approving budgets*: When your district is establishing its budget for the year—a public, annual process in communities

throughout the nation—you can ask that funds be allocated to advance climate mitigation, adaptation, and education. You can also ask for data on whether funding is being distributed and prioritized equitably for schools most likely to be impacted by climate change, including schools in low-income communities and communities of color.

- *School board elections*: Election season is an important opportunity to ensure that candidates are prioritizing and responding to climate-related issues. You can create forums and opportunities for candidates to talk about how they plan to address climate-driven events such as extreme heat, wildfire smoke, flooding, and other weather events that impact school closures, learning, and/or activities for students. You can also take action to ensure that school board candidates are engaged with the voices and views of young people in your community regarding climate action.
- *Facilities committee meetings*: Many school districts have public facilities or buildings committee meetings where school board and staff members discuss the status and priorities for the school district's infrastructure. These meetings can be powerful opportunities to learn, build relationships, and advocate for energy efficiency, decarbonization, and resilience for school buildings and grounds.

Step 5. Celebrate Successes and Lessons Learned Publicly, and Keep Going

Regularly report on progress made and lessons learned as part of your climate action efforts. Public reporting is a powerful tool for driving change within public entities. Consider including date-certain commitments for public progress reports in school board resolutions and policies. These reports can range from basic charts showing recent progress and next steps to more detailed analytics and performance indicators. By celebrating successes and sharing challenges openly, you can foster transparency and accountability in your climate action initiatives, inspiring others to join the cause. For example, DPS invested in a robust website and annual reports to celebrate and share the system's progress toward the commitments of their climate change action plan.[3] Anyone can access this website and see specific goals (like transitioning their school bus fleet to electric buses) and the progress toward those goals. Front and center on the home page are the broad categories of commitment and the positive economic impact of the district's sustainability measures.

PRACTITIONERS' REFLECTIONS ON LEADING CLIMATE ACTION IN SCHOOLS

Since our pivots to working on climate at the start of this decade, we have been leading and collaborating on advocacy for federal and state policy to support K–12 climate action, working with partners to create resources and tools for state and local leaders, and spreading awareness of the essential role for K–12 schools in addressing climate change. We started by telling our own pivot stories and now, having explored the issues, impacts, and practical steps, we want to share, on a more personal level, the ways that we have learned to make sense of our unfolding experience as advocates, policy entrepreneurs, and partners to decision makers about schools and climate.

In previous chapters, we suggested adopting key mind-sets about climate mitigation, adaptation, and education within schools. We now share a few guiding ideas rooted in reflection and distilled from our personal experiences leading this work. We offer them as coaching points for leaders without formal authority and as sparks for your approach as a change agent in your community.

Unapologetic Ambition

This is extraordinarily urgent work. It's okay to push up against people who think you might be asking for too much. It's sensible to ask for significant action and big change to reduce carbon pollution. Don't negotiate with yourself based on what you think might be feasible. Ask for what you and your community need and for what a livable future requires. Especially as someone who may be new to settings where decisions are made, the study of climate, the operation of school facilities, or all of these, it may be easier to defer to veteran leaders about the ambition, scale, direction, and pace of climate work. However, we won't know what's possible without making challenging demands of ourselves and our partners and pointing at unmistakable North Stars: date-certain decarbonization targets; adaptation to build resilience; and robust, relevant educational opportunities for students.

Risks will come with this territory. Risk can be daunting; but not acting is worse. It's better to try and learn, then try again. As pivoters, we have had to work to check our imposter syndrome or our occasional shock that *I'm the person!?* delivering a particular message or leading some piece of work. We've felt this in meetings with the White House, federal agencies, state and elected leaders, funders, and seasoned partners. In these moments, we strive to hold both humility and ambition at once. There is value in trying. Indeed, sometimes learning from past work and bringing a new perspective is what is needed to strengthen ambition or see solutions hiding in plain sight.

North Star Leadership

We don't and can't know all the steps from our current reality to our vision of a K–12 school system that has climate change education, adaptation, and mitigation at the core of its mission and operations. Complexity and ambiguity stretches all the way between where we are today and the future we all aspire to create. Change within education systems is always complex and often turbulent because participants hold diverse points of view on the ultimate priorities and the best path forward for students. The ground often shifts beneath us, and leaders need to support their teams and networks to hold fast to their North Stars while adjusting both strategy and tactics as the context changes.

North Star leadership means being clear where we are headed while remaining open about how we will get there and with whom. It means committing to steps that we know tap into the potential for change, although their actual results are uncertain and, in a sense, unknowable.

> Truly nimble organizations dare to create clarity at all times, even when they are not completely certain about whether it is correct. And if they later see a need to change course, they do so without hesitation or apology, and thus create clarity around the new idea or answer.
>
> —Patrick Lencioni, founder and president of the Table Group

Equity Imperative and Opportunity

Many of us working in education are dedicated to advancing equity, believing that quality education can provide a pathway to opportunities for historically marginalized students and communities. Despite efforts and intentions, however, inequitable structures persist within our education systems, from disparities in funding, resources, and expectations to unequal access to modern, healthy infrastructure, to uneven access to high-quality curricular offerings and instruction. These inequities disproportionately affect Black, Brown, Indigenous, and low-income students in rural or urban areas. We often hear people question our priorities, asking, "How can we make investments in climate action when basic infrastructure needs like repairing a leaky ceiling remain unaddressed?"

It's crucial to reposition climate action from being perceived as a nice-to-have to a must-have. Failing to do so will only exacerbate existing disparities in student health and educational opportunities. Students in low-income communities have the right to ride on electric buses without inhaling polluted air, to attend schools with comfortable learning environments free from extreme temperatures, and to explore career pathways in the burgeoning clean energy economy. By investing in these communities and supporting locally driven, community-developed initiatives, we can actively work toward addressing and mitigating long-standing inequities.

On the flip side, this moment could reinforce and exacerbate existing patterns of inequity. For example, today the federal Inflation Reduction Act (IRA) offers every school district robust incentives to deploy clean energy technologies in schools. Without an intentional approach, wealthier districts will lead on building electrification while poorer districts will continue to rely on aging fossil fuel equipment that locks in carbon pollution for several more decades and damages health and learning. This is a pivotal moment for us to prioritize equity and construct healthier, more resilient school systems that benefit all students.

Complexity Theory

No matter its size or setting, every school and district, and every agency at any level—county or state or federal—is a complex system. This means the school or district where you hope to catalyze climate action is a complex, emergent, dynamic system, too. An awareness of complexity theory will bolster your work leading change, so let us share some key ideas from complexity theory.[4]

Emergence is the idea that complex systems exhibit properties or behaviors that can't be easily predicted from looking at individual parts. For example, the behavior of a crowd at a stadium is emergent; it's not determined by any single person, although each person plays a role. As a result, small changes in complex systems can lead to disproportionately large effects. This means that cause-and-effect relationships aren't always linear or straightforward. Complexity scientists call this *nonlinearity*. It's like a small pebble causing ripples in a pond—the ripples grow much larger as they spread. For example, one public comment at a school board meeting that resonates with the right leader at the right time or a presentation to the district instructional leadership team might spark action in other parts of the district. We can't always know in advance the direction and magnitude of the reactions to and impacts of our actions.

Self-organization refers to the ability of complex systems to arrange or reconfigure themselves spontaneously without external control. This process often leads to the emergence of order, patterns, or structures from initially chaotic or disordered states. Think about how traffic flows or how an ecosystem adapts to changes over time. Feedback loops are mechanisms in which the output of a system feeds back into the system as input, influencing its behavior. Positive feedback loops amplify changes, potentially leading to instability, while negative feedback loops help maintain stability and equilibrium within the system.

One of the implications of this for Jonathan's work at UndauntedK12 is that he's wary of telling funders and partners, "If we do X, Y will happen" because he has learned that he often doesn't know how complex systems will respond to UndauntedK12's actions. Identifying desired outputs and outcomes is useful to guide direction, but they are always limited to our best thinking at a moment in time. It's important that leaders stay nimble as complex systems respond and move as a result of their efforts and as the dynamics change.

Simple, Complicated, and Complex Problems

The same book on systems change that taught Jonathan about complexity theory, *Getting to Maybe: How the World Is Changed* by Frances Westley, Brenda Zimmerman, and Michael Patton, also makes a point to differentiate among simple, complicated, or complex problems.[5] As you work for climate action, it will be important to consider what kind of problem you're working on to help you create a strategic path forward. Below we paraphrase *Getting to Maybe*'s description of each kind of problem and then provide illustrative examples of climate action in schools.

Baking a cake is a simple problem—no offense to bakers everywhere! Tested recipes are replicable. Expertise is not required, but experience increases the rate of success. A tested recipe produces nearly the same cake every time. We know there are not many simple problems in working for climate action in schools, but some do exist: for instance, switching to LED lights is a simple way schools can decrease their carbon footprint. To solve this straightforward problem, you will need to look at existing lighting, determine the lights that need to be switched, and make the switch. There are likely not as many variables in play as other climate action decisions.

Sending a rocket to the moon is complicated. You need specific expertise as well as rigid protocols or formulas. Key elements of the rocket *must* be identical to succeed. And then, theoretically, there is a high degree of certainty of outcome. Similarly, installing new charging stations for your school staff's electric vehicles is complex. You need to choose among technologies and products, ensure that your electrical service and transformers can handle the new load, choose technical partners, model the financials, and more. But if you work with expert contractors and partners, you can have a reasonably high degree of confidence in a positive project outcome.

Then there are complex challenges such as parenting. As parents ourselves, we immediately understand that raising a child is complex. Raising one child provides experience but is no guarantee of success with the next. Past experience with one of our older children helps but only when balanced with responsiveness to the specific needs of another child. Rigid protocols have a limited application or can be counterproductive.

Most climate action in schools involves complicated and complex problems. For example, implementing climate change lessons and content throughout the curriculum is at least a complicated problem for leaders with specific expertise and likely complex as you work with the diverse and idiosyncratic personalities and ask for behaviors to change. A pitfall to avoid is assuming that, because other schools or districts have done something before (i.e., installed charging infrastructure or solar panels), your project will be simple rather than complicated or complex.

Lessons from the Adoption Curve

The urgency and magnitude of climate action needs in schools demand that we develop strategies that support scale throughout the sector.

In 1962, Everett Rogers first coined the term "the adoption curve" to describe how technologies and ideas spread through societies over time, detailing the different stages of adoption by different groups of people.[6] Rogers envisioned the path of adoption existing on a bell curve, where the majority of individuals are in the middle and smaller segments are among the first and last to accept new ideas, technologies, and products. Jake Barton, a friend and collaborator, first suggested we consider how each segment of the adoption curve can help aspiring climate leaders identify what might motivate individuals in each group.

- *Innovators*: These are the individuals who are typically the first to embrace new ideas or technologies. They want to understand how the new thing works. Find the innovators within your context and support them to evangelize and bring their enthusiasm to the early adopters. Innovators might be excited to learn that electric heat pumps are as much as three hundred times more energy efficient as legacy, fossil fuel HVAC technologies. Or innovators might be the teachers who are excited about brainstorming, creating new lessons, and integrating climate science into their history, English, or math curriculum and courses.
- *Early adopters*: Early adopters are the visionaries. They are willing to take risks for breakthrough change. Early adopters are the participants in opportunities you create to pilot sustainability programs or initiatives. Early adopters also serve as advocates and champions for climate action within district and school communities, helping to generate momentum and enthusiasm for broader adoption. These might also be the people in your community who say yes to joining a small-group discussion to plan an advocacy campaign to replicate a model or practice from another district.
- *Early majority*: This group in the middle left of the curve tends to adopt new ideas or initiatives once they have been proven successful and are widely accepted by others. The early majority are the pragmatists—they are content to wait until others have adopted.

Maybe the new thing is just a fad. They want to hear from credible sources before they adopt. You can engage the early majority by showcasing successful examples of climate action initiatives implemented by innovators and early adopters. Evidence- and data-based case studies on the benefits of sustainability initiatives can help persuade this group to get involved. Leveraging existing community and labor networks and spaces can help you reach new "early majority" audiences with data and stories of earlier adopters.

- *Late majority*: The late majority in the middle right of the adoption curve adopts new ideas or initiatives only after most people have already accepted them. You can engage the late majority by emphasizing the social norms and expectations surrounding climate action within your district. Recognition programs, peer influence, and social pressure can be powerful motivators for encouraging the late majority to participate. Events to share testimonials from students about their motivations and experiences with climate education curriculum might motivate the late majority to get on board.
- *Laggards*: Laggards are typically the last to adopt new ideas or initiatives and may be resistant to change. They need clear explanations for how climate action benefits not only the environment but also the broader school community. Incentives, rewards, and requirements—carrots and sticks—can help overcome resistance from laggards.

By understanding where different technologies and aspects of climate action in schools fall on the adoption curve within your state or community context, you can tailor your efforts to engage and mobilize various segments of your district effectively. For example, Generation180, a national nonprofit that tracks the adoption of solar at schools across the country, reports that, although more and more schools install solar each year, as of the end of 2021, just 7 percent of schools nationwide generate their own solar energy.[7] Thus, in most markets, leaders and advocates are working to engage and persuade the "early adopters" who are generally more willing to take risks and pilot new programs or technologies. According to Rogers, drivers of adoption include factors such as perceived usefulness, ease of use, compatibility, observability, and trialability, which collectively influence individuals' decisions to adopt new technologies or innovations. Sharing case studies that describe the upfront and ongoing costs of previous projects and solar feasibility assessments can speak to these drivers and support adoption of solar in schools.

The percentage of schools that utilize modern heat pump technology to heat and cool buildings (rather than HVAC systems that burn fossil fuels) is even smaller than that of solar. Yet our goal needs to be widespread deployment of these modern HVAC systems throughout this decade. In this case, you will likely be targeting the "innovators," individuals interested in going deeper to understand the new or unfamiliar technologies. For example, as education leaders worked to address and improve indoor air quality in school buildings during and coming out of the COVID-19 pandemic, UndauntedK12 partnered with Rocky Mountain Institute, a clean energy think tank, to support school building decision makers in understanding and choosing modern, electric HVAC systems.[8]

Take a moment to consider the rates of adoption of the following aspects of climate action in your community's schools or in America's schools more broadly:

- Climate education integrated throughout the curriculum
- Clean energy career pathways
- Farm-to-school meals
- Heating and cooling all school buildings
- Electric kitchens
- Energy storage

In almost every case, you will be working with innovators and early adopters who need to be engaged and supported in embracing and implementing new practices, and who can then be among your most important allies in spreading and scaling climate action to the early and late majorities throughout our education systems.

Relationships and Partnerships

Trusting relationships are indispensable. The growing climate action community is an exceptional group of passionate, dedicated, creative, generous, determined people. There is rarely a project at UndauntedK12 or This Is Planet Ed that we don't do without partners. We can be undaunted, but we're not unlimited. For both of us, this means inviting other organizations to complement our small teams' expertise and capacity as collaborators on most projects. It means taking time for one-to-one conversations with partners new and old for periodic exchanges of perspective and updates on priorities. It means seeking input and feedback from diverse experts and perspectives before we share policy recommendations. It looks like creating ongoing coalitions and collaboration spaces to share and crowd-source wisdom and ensure that our actions make sense within a broader community of actors. As the saying goes: to go far, go together.

There are no shortcuts when it comes to relationships, no substitutes for investing the time to cultivate the trust that's necessary to collaborate and stand with diverse allies for significant change. The urgency you feel for action on climate will sometimes conflict with the time it takes to get to know people and understand the context that is essential for moving your work forward. By purposefully supporting allies and partners in shaping our collective vision of the desired future and of the pathways to achieving the vision, our coalitions can persevere through inevitable obstacles and setbacks.[9] The age-old wisdom rings true: change moves at the speed of trust.

Movement Building Mind-Sets

In our work for action and change, we draw on lessons and embrace tactics from community organizing traditions—both to drive success in our campaigns and to contribute momentum to the broader movement to secure a livable future. Community organizers often define power as the capacity to mobilize people and resources to effect change. In an organizing context, power is not seen solely as a hierarchical or top-down force but rather as something that emerges from the collective actions and relationships within a community. Power is seen as "organized people or organized money," emphasizing that it can stem from the unity and coordination of individuals or groups as well as from financial resources. This definition underscores the importance of grassroots mobilization, coalition building, and the amplification of voices traditionally marginalized in decision-making processes. True power lies in communities identifying their own needs, articulating their demands, and advocating for meaningful change.[10] Each of our organizations has built alliances and collaborates with base-building organizations that both shape our priorities and motivate decision makers to come to the table.

Organizers also understand that every campaign or action is an opportunity to develop leaders. As you plan meetings and steps in your campaign, sharing opportunities to take ownership and leadership will foster a sense of agency and responsibility within your crew. For example, if you were the speaker at the last school board meeting, you might encourage someone else to take a turn for the next event. Then both of you are veterans who can help more people use their voices! We cannot emphasize enough that people will come back and participate as they experience belonging, so cultivating a sense of community and inclusion can inspire long-term engagement and commitment.

Organizing tactics also embrace the ideas that "action is in the reaction" and that we need to adapt and refine our approaches (à la complexity theory) based on feedback and outcomes, continually evolving our strategies for maximum impact. In addition, every campaign or action is an opportunity to shape public narrative. Jonathan learned years ago from his participation with Oakland Community Organizations (now known as Faith in Action) that "a win is not a win unless it's public." We are intentional about putting time and resources into storytelling and communicating about what we're doing and why. This makes leaders and decision makers more accountable about following through on their commitments and can inspire others to join the movement.[11]

Timing, Cycles, Tenure, and Policy Windows

We also pay attention to leadership tenure, transitions, and the installation of new leadership within organizations. Policy, budget, and practice change often happens within two-, four-, and eight-year political cycles. Within every twenty-four-month cycle are shorter windows of intense election season activity, when action accelerates rapidly, like with the passage of the IRA, or when we need to shift strategy to be responsive to current dynamics. Framing problems in ways that bring people together and building a broad and diverse coalition of supporters can help you navigate inevitable leadership and political shifts.

And, finally, we are human beings with lives outside work—and so are our team members and partners. It is essential that we cultivate, nurture, exercise, and care for other parts of our human selves during the urgent pursuit of systemic change and climate action.

Leveraging Existing Frameworks, Tools, and Plans

While district-wide climate change action planning is a relatively new discipline, pursuing system-wide change and improvement is not. Leaders can leverage established frameworks for district-wide improvement—such as the Coherence Framework described in chapter 6—to drive climate action. The green schools movement, including the Center for Green Schools and the Green Schools National Network (GSNN), has also produced frameworks for districts and schools that can be helpful in supporting stakeholders to better understand how teaching and learning, district operations, district culture, and leadership will shift and support the core educational mission as we pursue action on climate.[12]

In addition, nonprofits such as SubjectToClimate, Ten Strands, North American Association of Environmental Education (NAAEE), Green Schoolyards America, and New Buildings Institute (NBI) regularly release new tools and resources to support districts with various aspects of climate action.[13] Sign up for their email lists!

As with anything else in education, we also encourage you to review, leverage, and borrow from the artifacts, plans, and processes of other districts. The UndauntedK12 and This Is Planet Ed websites include resources, tools, case studies, and model artifacts from schools and districts across the country.

Navigating Pushback

We think everyone can be won over to the work of addressing climate change. The future we aspire to create together is a better one for our children, schools, and communities. Who doesn't want cleaner air for all of us to breathe, more green spaces where our children play and learn, buildings that are comfortable when the weather is hot or cold, education that prepares students for the future they face?

Nonetheless, you may live in a community where action on climate change has become politicized, or you may encounter people within your community who are dismissive of climate action. This will affect your tactics as someone working to support action in your community—and it will color your experience. What does progress realistically look like in your school or your community? What steps, large or small, might eventually gain widespread support?

You might push for your district to take on a comprehensive planning process. Or the win in your community might be the development of a new career pathway that leads to good local jobs focused on clean energy technologies. The winning outcome might be to secure a commitment to leverage federal funds to purchase and pilot the district's first electric school buses. Your work might result in choosing a modern heat pump HVAC system for a new school building rather than an HVAC system that uses legacy technology and burns fossil fuels. Whichever approach you take and whatever objectives you set, there will undoubtedly be obstacles to your progress. You will need to be prepared for pushback and to support other leaders and allies as you work together to navigate your communities toward building a sustainable future.

Remember: "To care about climate change, we only have to be one thing: a human, living on planet earth."[14] Our climate is changing now. Our education systems must change too. We can harness this moment and shape a brighter future for all children and young people to come—when we work together. And there is no better place to start this work than in our schools.

Conclusion: A Reason for Hope

WORKING ON ISSUES related to climate change can take a toll. It means facing the multitude of negative climate impacts in daily life; watching the devastating realities in the news; or feeling isolated by the absence of sufficient dialogue among family, friends, colleagues, and political leaders. Not all days are easy or good. By the time this book is released, we know there will be new stories of climate impacts devastating students, families, schools, and communities. Many of these events will occur during the summer, a time that typically brings a sense of joy and happiness, which now, as of spring 2024, holds a looming sense of anxiety and fear. At times, the problem feels so big that nothing will ever right the course. Too often, we look at our children and feel guilty over decisions we make, like flying, or decisions our society makes, like extending a gas pipeline. So why should you have a reason for hope?

In these moments, we turn our attention to the other people working on climate change, people who are deeply committed to a livable future and bringing their passions, interests, and individual strengths to advance collective action. During the time it took to write this book, more students will have pushed their school districts to pass resolutions to develop climate change action plans; more educators will be engaging students in learning about our changing world; more school superintendents will recognize the realities of educational leadership in a changing climate and taking steps to build resilience; and more organizations, networks, and coalitions will recognize their opportunity to contribute to solutions.

We started this book discussing the stories of Vic, Maya, Naina, and Kiera: students who experienced their own climate awakenings and yet grew up with insufficient opportunities for climate learning in school. As teenagers, they faced obstacles and discouragement, yet that did not stop them from taking action. Now, as young adults, they are still working to shape a brighter future. In sharing their stories, we hope that you reflect on the role of education in these students' lives. Even with limited climate learning opportunities, their in-school and out-of-school learning helped shape them in finding their own paths. Creating spaces in school for students to grapple with climate challenges and engage with solutions can help maximize the catalytic potential of our work to shift our society. Let their stories inspire you to create more spaces for students so we can build lasting change to a brighter future together.

VIC

Motivated after learning about decision making during his afterschool program, Global Kids, Vic and his peers wanted to develop a campaign for action on climate change. But they worried that every idea they had would fall short. With only seven students, there weren't enough of them to make a dent in the climate fight. They needed more students to make a difference. To do that, it occurred to Vic that "young people need[ed] to know about this issue or understand the complexities of it." That was when they decided that this could be where they make a difference: "What if our campaign was to educate more young people?" Vic and his peers worked together to launch a citywide campaign for climate education in New York.

Vic then joined the Alliance for Climate Education (now Action for the Climate Emergency) as a fellow, where he learned more about campaigning and advocacy. He was asked to travel to Conference of the Parties (COP)21, a conference of global leaders on climate change, and then months later, Vic spoke before the UN, the place he had previously revered. During this speech, Vic talked about watching political leaders at COP engage in negotiations about "my future, something I honestly wish I didn't have to fight so hard to defend." He called on the leaders at the UN to build a better path forward.

> We have reached the moment in our history where we need to decide how much humanity means to us? How much do we mean to ourselves? In this the anthropocene, we must ensure that we are not characterized or held prisoner by the mistakes of the past, but that we are defined by the perseverance and bravery of the present. Join young people around the world in celebrating the best possible version of our future.

Despite Vic's high level of activism, he was disheartened by the process and the lack of space for young people to have a meaningful role in the conversation. After meeting with countless political leaders and their staff, Vic felt "kind of ignored and kind of patronized." He added, "I just was feeling a lot of frustration, you know, having to call people all the time just [getting] photo ops and pats on the back, but no real difference because, I guess in their head, I didn't have a stake in the position of power that they were holding." At that point, Vic began working with Our Children's Trust and made the decision to join as a plaintiff in *Juliana et al. v. United States of America et al.*, a lawsuit where a group of young plaintiffs are suing the federal government, asserting that it violated their rights by failing to act on climate change and reduce emissions. Vic's case is not a singular event; in the summer of 2023, in the constitutional court case *Held v. State of Montana*, sixteen young people successfully argued that Montana violated their state constitutional right to a "clean and healthful environment" by promoting the burning of fossil fuels—the main contributor to climate change.

Vic, in considering how climate change will impact his professional decisions in the future, said, "I don't think I'll ever be able to stop prioritizing it."

MAYA

In her public magnet art school in Charleston, South Carolina, Maya enrolled in a creative writing program that offered her an "unusual amount of freedom" to write about her interests. Maya said that the program helped her see "writing as a tool" for exploration "and even [as] a tool to create social change." She was able to engage meaningfully with a group of her peers and they were "finding ways to use their voices and use words to really tell the narratives that weren't being told."

Maya applied for a national journalism fellowship with Student Voice, a youth-led national nonprofit organization aimed at empowering students as storytellers, organizers, and partners to advocate for solutions to educational inequity. This fellowship intended to build a community of writers sharing their own experiences to improve educational opportunities. Maya wrote a piece titled "Remaining Inclusive in the Fight for Environmental Justice" that highlighted how the historical inequities and racial divides in Charleston have resulted in current environmental inequities. She emphasized that thinking about solutions must take this intersectional frame into account:

> Frequently pummeled by the hurricanes that assault the Carolina coast and situated on the very edge of a rising sea level, Charleston is primed to be one of the first cities to face the environmental issues anticipated for the world in the coming decades. As this occurs, however, the city cannot forget that its natural and social environments do not exist separately from one another. One affects the other, and time will only tell

whether the city will crumble under the waves, or rise to the upcoming challenges with innovation, inclusivity, and Southern grace.

Maya described climate change as a "main motivating factor" in what she studied in college. In fact, in her college application essay, she emphasized her interest in exploring "how to bring people into thinking about climate change in productive ways." At Stanford University, she entered an interdisciplinary urban studies program, where she was able to consider intersectional issues—climate, sustainability, community engagement, the economy, and urban design.

During high school, Maya always thought about climate change as science given that was how she was exposed to it in school. This had left her discouraged. "I really care about climate, but I don't want to be a scientist." But now she sees different potential paths for herself. She is considering journalism or urban planning, but she indicated that whatever "field I go into, the issue that I'll be thinking about is climate and climate equity and how to make something that feels really hopeless or something that seems really hopeless, feel less hopeless in terms of individuals taking action."

NAINA

As a tenth grader with the Sunrise Movement, an organization that advocates for political action climate change, Naina organized a climate strike in her hometown of Ann Arbor, Michigan. Even though she saw the strikes as a powerful tool, leaving school to do something about climate change seemed a little strange to her. "We want to do something about climate change. We have to leave school. . . . We had so few avenues to take climate action in school that our primary outlet for this issue that we cared about was the opposite. It was outside of school."

Going into eleventh grade, Naina shifted to a national role representing the Sunrise Movement on the Climate Coalition to help organize strikes, including the large youth strike that occurred September 20, 2019. For many of these strikes, the youth groups saw this as an opportunity to learn about climate justice. They would bring in speakers to talk about lived experiences or experts to discuss solutions. Naina reflected, "I think that really demonstrates how much hunger there was among people in my generation, for more information, more opportunity to digest the set of issues, more opportunity to talk about solutions, and just more dialogue."

Recognizing this need, Naina helped to start the middle and high school support team within the Sunrise Movement's national infrastructure. The goal of the support team was to engage more middle and high school students within the Sunrise Movement and help them build the knowledge and skills needed to advance action locally. The support team ran trainings for middle and high school students focused on what Naina described as "hard skills as well as more historical and theoretical knowledge." They would focus on hard skills such as how to run an effective meeting, build a coalition, or hold a one-on-one conversation. Based on history and theoretical frameworks, they would discuss solutions to the climate crisis and efforts like the Green New Deal and how it compared to the New Deal in the 1930s and other attempts at social transformation. This work helped Naina feel, as she put it, "empowered."

> I always really respected authority growing up. It led me to have a lot of really positive relationships with my teachers, my educators, my school administrators, and I still feel positive about all of that today. But there was something really empowering about taking things into our own hands, as young people and saying, "Well, we don't actually need an older generation to turn the cogs of bureaucracy and change the school curriculum and institute standards in the classroom that will enable us to talk about all of these issues. We can actually just learn about them ourselves, and then spread information about them ourselves." I still think that shouldn't be how it has to be. It should be

accessible to everyone via the classroom. But in the absence of that, it was really empowering to do it on your own.

At Yale University, Naina remains broadly interested in climate change and particularly in environmental law. She is learning holistically about how environmental law can help people recover from climate disasters, hold responsible parties accountable, or support activists in "disrupting business as usual to call attention to the issue." Naina is majoring in history, and she is interested in learning from the past about both failed and successful efforts for societal transformation, with societal transformation being "what we're tasked with in the face of the climate crisis."

When asked about how climate change might impact what she decides to do professionally in the future, Naina emphatically stated, "I can't imagine doing any work that doesn't grapple with climate in some way." She added, "Both in terms of professional choices and in terms of lifestyle choices, I think climate will impact my future forever."

KIERA

When Kiera moved from Alaska to Massachusetts to attend Harvard University, she realized she was from a "more crunchy background" than many of her classmates. Fortunately, she was able to make connections with others from the Pacific Northwest given their bonds over being "very outdoorsy." Kiera and many of these classmates joined Harvard's Republican Club. By her sophomore year, Kiera was president.

Kiera quickly realized that climate change was perceived as a partisan issue. This "didn't make a lot of intuitive sense." She added, "I care a lot about being able to go skiing, being able to go hiking and not be sweltering, and to go fishing and have a normal season." But in talking to other students within her political circles, rather than staunch opposition, she heard mostly the following from people, "I don't know, don't ask me about that, I don't have answers, I don't have thoughts."

Acknowledging the need to increase dialogue—not just about the problem but also about supporting solutions—Kiera connected with some peers to build an effort with the goal of supporting student leaders from both sides of the aisle and from colleges across the country to advocate for specific consensus climate solutions. In 2018, this group of student leaders launched Students for Carbon Dividends (S4CD), a bipartisan nonprofit aimed at advocating for carbon dividends as a climate solution.

Trying to bring young Republicans to this bipartisan effort was not as straightforward as she had initially hoped. She noted, "It's really the right side of the aisle that has a longer way to go on even just starting the dialogue." To foster more conversation about climate change among Republicans, in 2019, Kiera founded Young Conservatives for Carbon Dividends (YCCD). The 501c(4) advocacy organization brought together young Republicans from colleges across the country to push Republican political leaders to support carbon dividends and recognize the Republican Party's legacy of environmental leadership.

Kiera took a class called Startup Research and Development that was "incredibly impactful" in helping her build the skills she needed to start YCCD. In every class, Kiera and her peers were required to share how they had advanced their start-up over the previous week. She grappled with questions such as: How do I hire people? How do I offer health care? How do I attract a team that is mission driven and equally motivated to what I'm doing while still maintaining a healthy work, life balance? The course created a community of entrepreneurs who, despite working on different projects, shared ideas, challenges, and opportunities to get an organization off the ground.

When she entered college and given her environmental interests, Kiera thought she would have pursued biology, but she pivoted. "I pretty quickly realized that my value add was [going to] be on the policy side." The questions that were driving her thinking demand systemic and policy answers. How big is this problem? What actions are available to even start to tackle this? Who is organizing people on this? How are they being organized? What governing bodies see themselves as being responsible for this? As a result of these questions, Kiera's career has focused on policy, climate change, and clean energy. After leaving YCCD, Kiera worked in Washington, DC, on environmental policy and then shifted to work in policy with an offshore wind company to help grow the industry. Kiera has advice for others entering this work:

> There are a lot of climate organizations out there. But if there's one that doesn't fit your niche, create it. I think there's a lot of pressure the other way. Where it's like, "Well, you can just join one of these larger umbrella organizations which are doing great work." But if there is a niche problem that you feel uniquely positioned to work on—go for it.

Vic, Maya, Naina, and Kiera are persistent, committed, and passionate. Despite not having ample space to learn about climate change in school, they used their educational experiences and opportunities to develop paths to action, learning from and relying on others along the way. They are not following the same path; they are following their own unique paths to advance our common good. And they aren't the only ones. This book is filled with stories of people who bring their knowledge, skills, and passions to the climate fight. This is what we need more of—action. Students should not have to sue the government or strike from school to see adults taking action. All young people across the country have the potential to bring their interests, strengths, and passions to this work, and educators can unlock that potential in schools.

As pivoters toward climate after decades-long careers in education and as parents today, we still have many moments of overwhelm and grief thinking about the future—what's ahead for us and our children and all that needs to be done. But we also challenge ourselves to look at our situation in another way: What if we were born at just the right time? What if all of us today have the opportunity to collaboratively build a brighter future and that this is our moment to seize?

On the power of education, Nelson Mandela remarked, "Education is the most powerful weapon which you can use to change the world." As educators, we can bring what we know to advance "the best possible version of our future," and we can ensure that our students know what they can do as well. We can support more young people like Kiera, Naina, Maya, and Vic in building their paths to action and thus enable them to thrive in a changing climate. We can empower more people to bring their unique perspectives to advance solutions collaboratively. Our collective potential is a reason for hope.

NOTES

INTRODUCTION

1. Katharine Hayhoe, "In the Face of Climate Change, We Must Act So That We Can Feel Hopeful—Not the Other Way Around," *Time*, August 12, 2021, https://time.com/6089999/climate-change-hope/.
2. K12 Climate Action Commission, "K12 Climate Action Commission Motivation," 2021, https://www.thisisplaneted.org/resources/climate-action-plan-2021.
3. Potential Energy Coalition, *Global Report: Later Is Too Late* (New York: Potential Energy Coalition, 2023), https://potentialenergycoalition.org/guides-and-reports/global-report/.
4. Ayana Elizabeth Johnson and Katharine K. Wilkinson, eds., *All We Can Save: Truth, Courage, and Solutions for the Climate Crisis* (New York: One World, 2020).
5. Intergovernmental Panel on Climate Change, *Global Warming of 1.5°C* (Geneva: Intergovernmental Panel on Climate Change, 2018), https://www.ipcc.ch/sr15/.
6. This Is Planet Ed, "This Is Planet Ed," Aspen Institute, 2024, https://www.thisisplaneted.org/.
7. Merriam-Webster.com Dictionary, s.v. "undaunted," accessed July 24, 2024, https://www.merriam-webster.com/dictionary/undaunted.
8. Adam B. Smith, "2022 U.S. Billion-Dollar Weather and Climate Disasters in Historical Context," Beyond the Data, NOAA Climate.gov, January 10, 2023, https://www.climate.gov/news-features/blogs/beyond-data/2022-us-billion-dollar-weather-and-climate-disasters-historical.

CHAPTER 1

1. Caroline Hickman et al., "Climate Anxiety in Children and Young People and Their Beliefs About Government Responses to Climate Change: A Global

Survey," *Lancet* 5, no. 12 (December 2021), Figure 1, https://doi.org/10.1016/S2542-5196(21)00278-3.

2. Susan Clayton et al., "Mental Health and Our Changing Climate: Impacts, Implications, and Guidance," American Psychological Association, Climate for Health, and ecoAmerica, March 2017, apa.org/news/press/releases/2017/03/mental-health-climate.pdf.
3. "IPCC, 2023: Summary for Policymakers," in *Climate Change 2023: Synthesis Report. Contribution of Working Groups I, II and III to the Sixth Assessment Report of the Intergovernmental Panel on Climate Change,* ed. H. Lee and J. Romero (Geneva, Switzerland: IPCC, 2023), 1–34, https://www.ipcc.ch/report/ar6/syr/downloads/report/IPCC_AR6_SYR_SPM.pdf.
4. Probable Futures is a nonprofit climate literacy initiative that makes tools, stories, and resources available to everyone, everywhere. See https://probablefutures.org/.
5. António Guterres, "Opinion: Amid Backsliding on Climate, the Renewables Effort Now Must Be Tripled," *Washington Post,* April 4, 2022, https://www.washingtonpost.com/opinions/2022/04/04/new-ipcc-climate-report-on-averting-catastrophe/.
6. Katharine Wilkinson, "The Climate Crisis Is a Call to Action: These 5 Steps Helped Me Figure Out How to Be of Use," *Time,* July 19, 2021, https://time.com/6071765/what-can-i-do-to-fight-climate-change/.
7. Ilona M. Otto et al., "Social Tipping Dynamics for Stabilizing Earth's Climate by 2050," *Proceedings of the National Academy of Sciences* 117, no. 5 (January 2020), https://doi.org/10.1073/pnas.190057711.
8. Madeline Will and Arianna Prothero, "Teens Know Climate Change Is Real: They Want Schools to Teach More About It," *Education Week,* November 21, 2022, https://www.edweek.org/teaching-learning/teens-know-climate-change-is-real-they-want-schools-to-teach-more-about-it/2022/11.
9. Kanyinke Sena, "Recognizing Indigenous Peoples' Land Interests Is Critical for People and Nature," *World Wildlife Fund,* October 22, 2020, https://www.worldwildlife.org/stories/recognizing-indigenous-peoples-land-interests-is-critical-for-people-and-nature.
10. Ivy Morgan, "Equal Is Not Good Enough," *Education Trust,* November 30, 2022, https://edtrust.org/resource/equal-is-not-good-enough/.
11. Candace Jackson, "What Is Redlining?," *New York Times,* August 17, 2021, https://www.nytimes.com/2021/08/17/realestate/what-is-redlining.html.
12. Office of Minority Health, "Asthma and African Americans," Office of Minority Health, US Department of Health & Human Services, https://minorityhealth.hhs.gov/asthma-and-african-americans.
13. United States Government Accountability Office, *Disaster Recovery: School Districts in Socially Vulnerable Communities Faced Heightened Challenges after Recent Natural Disasters,* United States Government Accountability Office,

GAO-22-104606, January 2022, https://www.gao.gov/assets/gao-22-104606.pdf.

14. Rene, "Ketchikan Alaska Weather: What to Expect During Your Visit," *Experience Ketchikan*, https://www.experienceketchikan.com/Ketchikan-Alaska-weather.html.
15. Washington Post/Kaiser Family Foundation, "Climate Change Survey," *Washington Post*, July 9–August 5, 2019, https://www.washingtonpost.com/context/washington-post-kaiser-family-foundation-climate-change-survey-july-9-aug-5-2019/601ed8ff-a7c6-4839-b57e-3f5eaa8ed09f/?itid=lk_inline_manual_5.
16. New Jersey Department of Education, "Climate Change Education by Grade Band," Department of Education, Official Site of the State of New Jersey, January 2, 2024, https://www.nj.gov/education/standards/climate/learning/gradeband/.
17. Tammy Murphy, "Education Is Our Greatest Weapon Against Climate Change," This Is Planet Ed, Aspen Institute, https://www.thisisplaneted.org/blog/education-is-our-greatest-weapon-against-climate-change.
18. Jason Horowitz, "Italy's Students Will Get a Lesson in Climate Change: Many Lessons, in Fact," *New York Times*, November 5, 2019, https://www.nytimes.com/2019/11/05/world/europe/italy-schools-climate-change.html.
19. Alexander Rabin and Lisa Patel, "Opinion, Guest Essay: Our Children's Lungs Are Uniquely Vulnerable to All This Wildfire Smoke," *New York Times*, July 2, 2023, https://www.nytimes.com/2023/07/02/opinion/wildfire-smoke-air-quality-kids-children-health.html.
20. Troy Closson, "Schools in the Northeast Cancel Recess and Close Early as Air Quality Worsens," *New York Times*, June 7, 2023, https://www.nytimes.com/2023/06/07/nyregion/air-quality-schools-recess-north-east.html.
21. Rosana Aguilera et al., "Fine Particles in Wildfire Smoke and Pediatric Respiratory Health in California," *Pediatrics* 147, no. 4 (April 2021), https://doi.org/10.1542/peds.2020-027128.
22. Gina Jiménez, "ER Visits for Asthma in New York City Soared as Wildfire Smoke Blanketed the Region," *Inside Climate News*, June 14, 2023, https://insideclimatenews.org/news/14062023/new-york-er-asthma-willdfire-smoke/.
23. Erin Digitale, "5 Questions: Lisa Patel on California Wildfires and School Ventilation," Stanford Medicine, July 29, 2021, https://med.stanford.edu/news/all-news/2021/07/lisa-patel-on-california-wildfires-and-school-ventilation.html.

CHAPTER 2

1. Yale Program on Climate Change Communication (YPCCC), *Five Facts, Ten Words*, February 2021, https://climatecommunication.yale.edu/wp-content/uploads/2021/02/Five-Facts-Ten-Words.pdf.

2. National Oceanic and Atmospheric Administration (NOAA), "Carbon Dioxide Now More Than 50% Higher Than Pre-Industrial Levels," June 3, 2022, https://www.noaa.gov/news-release/carbon-dioxide-now-more-than-50-higher-than-pre-industrial-levels.
3. NOAA, "Carbon Dioxide Now More Than 50% Higher."
4. NASA, "Carbon Dioxide Hits New High," Global Climate Change, July 16, 2013, https://climate.nasa.gov/climate_resources/7/graphic-carbon-dioxide-hits-new-high/.
5. Intergovernmental Panel on Climate Change (IPCC), *AR6 Synthesis Report: Climate Change 2023,* March 2023, https://www.ipcc.ch/report/sixth-assessment-report-cycle/.
6. Kelly Levin, "Half a Degree and a World Apart: The Difference in Climate Impacts Between 1.5°C and 2°C of Warming," World Resources Institute, October 7, 2018, https://www.wri.org/insights/half-degree-and-world-apart-difference-climate-impacts-between-15c-and-2c-warming.
7. David I. Armstrong McKay et al., "Exceeding 1.5°C Global Warming Could Trigger Multiple Climate Tipping Points," *Science* 377, no. 6611 (2022), https://www.science.org/doi/10.1126/science.abn7950.
8. Joseph Stromberg, "What Is the Anthropocene and Are We in It?," *Smithsonian Magazine,* January 2013, https://www.smithsonianmag.com/science-nature/what-is-the-anthropocene-and-are-we-in-it-164801414/.
9. Niels de Hoog et al., "How Has the World's Population Grown Since 1950?," *Guardian,* November 14, 2022, https://www.theguardian.com/global-development/ng-interactive/2022/nov/14/how-has-the-worlds-population-grown-since-1950.
10. Intergovernmental Panel on Climate Change (IPCC), "Summary for Policymakers," in *Climate Change 2022: Mitigation of Climate Change. Contribution of Working Group III to the Sixth Assessment Report of the Intergovernmental Panel on Climate Change,* ed. P. R. Shukla et al. (Cambridge: Cambridge University Press, 2023), https://doi.org/10.1017/9781009157926.001; United States Environmental Protection Agency, "Inventory of U.S. Greenhouse Gas Emissions and Sinks," updated April 11, 2024, https://www.epa.gov/ghgemissions/inventory-us-greenhouse-gas-emissions-and-sinks.
11. Johannes Friedrich et al., "This Interactive Chart Shows Changes in the World's Top Emitters," World Resources Institute, March 2, 2023, https://www.wri.org/insights/interactive-chart-shows-changes-worlds-top-10-emitters.
12. United States Environmental Protection Agency, "Sources of Greenhouse Gas Emissions," updated June 5, 2024, https://www.epa.gov/ghgemissions/sources-greenhouse-gas-emissions.
13. Intergovernmental Panel on Climate Change (IPCC), "Summary for Policymakers," in *Climate Change 2022: Impacts, Adaptation and Vulnerability. Contribution of Working Group II to the Sixth Assessment Report of the Intergovernmental*

Panel on Climate Change, ed. H.-O. Pörtner et al. (Cambridge: Cambridge University Press, 2023), 3–33, https://doi.org/10.1017/9781009325844.001.

14. Sarah Kaplan, "Floods, Fires, and Deadly Heat Are the Alarm Bells of a Planet on the Brink," *Washington Post,* July 13, 2023, https://www.washingtonpost.com/climate-environment/2023/07/12/climate-change-flooding-heat-wave-continue/.
15. Matthew Cappucci, "Unforgiving Heat Wave Forecast in Swaths of the U.S. in Coming Days," *Washington Post,* July 12, 2023, https://www.washingtonpost.com/weather/2023/07/12/heat-wave-forecast-arizona-texas-southwest/.
16. Zach St. George, "He Wrote a Gardening Column. He Ended Up Documenting Climate Change," *New York Times,* July 28, 2021, https://www.nytimes.com/2021/07/28/magazine/gardening-column-climate-change.html.
17. United States Environmental Protection Agency (EPA), *Climate Change and Children's Health and Well-Being in the United States,* April 2023, https://www.epa.gov/system/files/documents/2023-04/CLiME_Final%20Report.pdf.
18. World Meteorological Organization, "Past Eight Years Confirmed to Be the Warmest on Record," January 12, 2023, https://wmo.int/news/media-centre/past-eight-years-confirmed-be-eight-warmest-record.
19. World Meteorological Organization, *State of the Global Climate 2023,* March 19, 2024, https://library.wmo.int/records/item/68835-state-of-the-global-climate-2023.
20. United States Environmental Protection Agency, "Climate Change Indicators: Heat Waves," updated June 27, 2024, https://www.epa.gov/climate-indicators/climate-change-indicators-heat-waves.
21. IPCC, "Summary for Policymakers."
22. Austyn Gaffney, "Seeking Stability in School When the Flood Waters Rise," *Washington Post,* October 21, 2022, https://www.washingtonpost.com/education/2022/10/21/kentucky-flooding-school-disasters/.
23. Brody Adams, "By the Numbers: A Look Back on California's Historic Heatwave," *ABC10 Sacramento,* September 12, 2022, https://www.abc10.com/article/weather/california-heatwave-in-numbers/103-c7325ee0-324d-4a18-8001-4d81dd6dc14a.
24. Thomas Kika, "Western States Send Kids Home Early as Heat Wave Scorches," *Newsweek,* September 7, 2022, https://www.newsweek.com/western-states-send-kids-home-early-heat-wave-scorches-california-colorado-1740421.
25. René Marsh, "Extreme Weather Has Devastated Schools Around the Country. Now Their Students Are Suffering," *CNN,* October 17, 2022, https://www.cnn.com/2022/10/17/us/extreme-weather-schools-hurricane-ian-climate.
26. Brady Dennis and Sarah Kaplan, "Jackson, Miss., Shows How Extreme Weather Can Trigger a Clean-Water Crisis," *Washington Post,* August 31, 2022, https://www.washingtonpost.com/climate-environment/2022/08/31/jackson-water-crisis-mississippi-floods/.

27. Cory Turner, "Water Systems Failures in Jackson, Miss., Force Schools to Return to Remote Learning," *NPR*, September 2, 2022, https://www.npr.org/2022/09/02/1120798658/water-systems-failures-in-jackson-miss-force-schools-to-return-to-remote-learnin.
28. Sarah Schwartz, "Digging Deeper into the Stark Declines on NAEP: 5 Things to Know," *Education Week*, September 2, 2022, https://www.edweek.org/leadership/digging-deeper-into-the-stark-declines-on-naep-5-things-to-know/2022/09; Emma Goldberg, "Teens in Covid Isolation: 'I Felt Like I Was Suffocating,'" *New York Times*, October 5, 2021, https://www.nytimes.com/2020/11/12/health/covid-teenagers-mental-health.html; US Government Accountability Office, *K–12 Education: An Estimated 1.1 Million Teachers Nationwide Had At Least One Student Who Never Showed Up for Class in the 2020–21 School Year*, March 23, 2022, https://www.gao.gov/assets/gao-22-104581.pdf.
29. Bruce Bekker et al., "Association of Air Pollution and Heat Exposure with Preterm Birth, Low Birth Weight, and Stillbirth in the US: A Systematic Review," *JAMA Network Open* 3, no. 6 (2020), https://jamanetwork.com/journals/jamanetworkopen/fullarticle/2767260.
30. Emilia Basilio et al., "Wildfire Smoke Exposure During Pregnancy: A Review of Potential Mechanisms of Placental Toxicity, Impact on Obstetric Outcomes, and Strategies to Reduce Exposure," *International Journal of Environmental Research and Public Health* 19, no. 21 (November 2022), https://doi.org/10.3390/ijerph192113727; Anne R. Waldrop et al., "Antenatal Wildfire Smoke Exposure and Hypertensive Disorders of Pregnancy," *American Journal of Obstetrics & Gynecology* 228, no. 1 (January 2023), https://doi.org/10.1016/j.ajog.2022.11.082.
31. Cornelieke S. H. Aarnoudse-Moens et al., "Meta-Analysis of Neurobehavioral Outcomes in Very Preterm and/or Very Low Birth Weight Children," *Pediatrics* 124, no. 2 (2009), https://publications.aap.org/pediatrics/article-abstract/124/2/717/72345/Meta-Analysis-of-Neurobehavioral-Outcomes-in-Very?redirectedFrom=fulltext; Linda D. Breeman et al., "Preterm Cognitive Function into Adulthood," *Pediatrics* 136, no. 3 (2015), https://publications.aap.org/pediatrics/article-abstract/136/3/415/61222/Preterm-Cognitive-Function-Into-Adulthood?redirectedFrom=fulltext.
32. Center for Climate, Health, and the Global Environment, "Reducing Asthma by Tackling the Climate Crisis," Harvard T. H. Chan School of Public Health, https://www.hsph.harvard.edu/c-change/subtopics/climate-change-and-asthma/.
33. Centers for Disease Control and Prevention (CDC), "Most Recent National Asthma Data," November 21, 2022, https://www.cdc.gov/asthma/most_recent_national_asthma_data.htm.
34. William R. L. Anderegg et al., "Anthropogenic Climate Change Is Worsening North American Pollen Season," *Proceedings of the National Academy*

of Sciences 118, no. 7 (February 2021), https://www.pnas.org/doi/10.1073/pnas.2013284118.

35. Sara B. Johnson et al., "Asthma and Attendance in Urban Schools," *Preventing Chronic Disease* 16 (2019), https://www.cdc.gov/pcd/issues/2019/19_0074.htm.
36. Center for Climate, Health, and the Global Environment, "Climate Change, Heatwaves, and Health," Harvard T. H. Chan School of Public Health, https://www.hsph.harvard.edu/c-change/subtopics/climate-change-heatwaves-and-health.
37. Center for Climate, Health, and the Global Environment, "Climate Change & Child's Developing Brain," Harvard T. H. Chan School of Public Health, https://www.hsph.harvard.edu/c-change/subtopics/climate-change-and-a-childs-brain/.
38. United States Environmental Protection Agency, "Climate Change and the Health of Indigenous Populations," updated December 27, 2023, https://www.epa.gov/climate-change/climate-change-and-health-indigenous-populations.
39. Centers for Disease Control and Prevention (CDC), "Adverse Childhood Experiences," April 9, 2024, https://www.cdc.gov/violenceprevention/aces/index.html.
40. Jose G. C. Laurent et al., "Reduced Cognitive Function During a Heat Wave Among Residents of Non-Air-Conditioned Buildings: An Observational Study of Young Adults in the Summer of 2016," *PLoS Medicine* 15, no. 7 (July 2018), https://doi.org/10.1371/journal.pmed.1002605.
41. R. Jisung Park et al., "Heat and Learning," *American Economic Journal: Economic Policy* 12, no. 2 (May 2020), https://www.aeaweb.org/articles?id=10.1257%2Fpol.20180612.
42. EPA, *Climate Change and Children's Health.*
43. Trust for Public Land, *School's Out: A Trust for Public Land Special Report,* August 2020, https://www.tpl.org/wp-content/uploads/2020/08/Schools-Out_A-Trust-for-Public-Land-Special-Report.pdf.
44. Lily Katz, "A Racist Past, a Flooded Future: Formerly Redlined Areas Have $107 Billion Worth of Homes Facing High Flood Risk—25% More Than Non-Redlined Areas," *Redfin News,* June 23, 2021, https://www.redfin.com/news/redlining-flood-risk/.
45. Trust for Public Land, *The Heat Is On: A Trust for Public Land Special Report,* September 2020, https://www.tpl.org/wp-content/uploads/2020/09/The-Heat-is-on_A-Trust-for-Public-Land_special-report_r1_2.pdf.
46. Marissa Hauptman et al., "Proximity to Major Roadways and Asthma Symptoms in the School Inner-City Asthma Study," *Journal of Allergy and Clinical Immunology* 145, no. 1 (January 2020), https://www.ncbi.nlm.nih.gov/pmc/articles/PMC6949366/.

47. Ayurella Horn-Muller, "Alaskan Tribal Communities Confront Food Insecurity After Storm," *Axios*, September 23, 2022, https://www.axios.com/2022/09/23/alaskan-tribal-communities-storm.
48. Pew Charitable Trusts, "Flooding Threatens Public Schools Across the Country," August 1, 2017, https://www.pewtrusts.org/en/research-and-analysis/issue-briefs/2017/08/flooding-threatens-public-schools-across-the-country.
49. US Government Accountability Office, *Disaster Recovery: School Districts in Socially Vulnerable Communities Faced Heightened Challenges After Recent Natural Disasters*, January 2022, https://www.gao.gov/assets/gao-22-104606.pdf.
50. IPCC, "Summary for Policymakers."
51. UNICEF, *The Climate Crisis Is a Child Rights Crisis: Introducing the Children's Climate Risk Index*, 2021, https://www.unicef.org/reports/climate-crisis-child-rights-crisis.
52. Charlotte Alter, Suyin Haynes, and Justin Worland, "TIME 2019 Person of the Year: Greta Thunberg," *TIME*, December 4, 2019, https://time.com/person-of-the-year-2019-greta-thunberg/.
53. Alter, Haynes, and Worland, "TIME 2019 Person of the Year."
54. New Buildings Institute, "Getting to Zero in Schools," https://newbuildings.org/nbi-key-markets/getting-to-zero-in-schools/.
55. Emma Hines and Sara Ross, *HVAC Choices for Student Health and Learning*, UndauntedK12, January 2023, https://www.undauntedk12.org/hvac-rmi.
56. Probable Futures is a nonprofit climate literacy initiative that makes tools, stories, and resources available to everyone, everywhere, at https://probablefutures.org/.
57. This Is Planet Ed and Capita, "Think of the Children: The Young and Future Generations Drive U.S. Climate Concern," October 25, 2022, Aspen Institute, https://www.thisisplaneted.org/blog/think-of-the-children-the-young-and-future-generations-drive-u-s-climate-concern.

CHAPTER 3

1. Tammy Synder Murphy, "Education Is Our Greatest Weapon Against Climate Change," This Is Planet Ed, Aspen Institute, https://www.thisisplaneted.org/blog/education-is-our-greatest-weapon-against-climate-change.
2. Murphy, "Education Is Our Greatest Weapon."
3. New Jersey School Boards Association, "New Jersey Establishes Office of Climate Education," *School Board Notes* 47, no. 9 (September 26, 2023), https://www.njsba.org/news-publications/school-board-notes/september-26-2023-vol-xlvii-no-9/new-jersey-establishes-first-in-the-nation-office-of-climate-change-education/.
4. Murphy, "Education Is Our Greatest Weapon."
5. K12 Climate Action, "State Policy Landscape 2020," This Is Planet Ed, Aspen Institute, https://www.thisisplaneted.org/blog/state-policy-landscape-2020.

6. This Is Planet Ed and Capita, "Think of the Children: The Young and Future Generations Drive U.S. Climate Concern," This Is Planet Ed, Aspen Institute, https://www.thisisplaneted.org/blog/think-of-the-children-the-young-and-future-generations-drive-u-s-climate-concern.
7. North American Association for Environmental Education, "The State of Climate Change Education: Findings from a National Survey of Educators," October 2022, https://eepro.naaee.org/learning/climate-change-education-what-are-we-hearing-educators-and-administrators.
8. Anthony Leiserowitz et al., "Climate Note: Global Warming's Six Americas, Fall 2023," *Yale Program on Climate Change Communication,* December 14, 2023, https://climatecommunication.yale.edu/publications/global-warmings-six-americas-fall-2023/.
9. This Is Planet Ed, "Higher Ed Listening Session VI," This Is Planet Ed, Aspen Institute, https://www.thisisplaneted.org/resources/higher-ed-listening-session-vi.
10. Katie Worth, *Miseducation: How Climate Change Is Taught in America* (New York: Columbia Global Reports, 2021).
11. Jill Anderson, "How Climate Change Is Taught in America," *Edcast,* Harvard Graduate School of Education, November 12, 2021, https://www.gse.harvard.edu/ideas/edcast/21/11/how-climate-change-taught-america.
12. National Center for Science Education and Texas Freedom Network Education Fund, *Making the Grade? How State Public School Science Standards Address Climate Change,* States at a Glance, October 2020, https://climategrades.org/#data.
13. K12 Climate Action, "Listening Session IV: How Can Schools Support Teaching and Learning to Address Climate Change," This Is Planet Ed, Aspen Institute, https://www.thisisplaneted.org/blog/listening-session-iv-teaching-and-learning-climate-change.
14. "About PolarTREC," PolarTREC, https://www.polartrec.com/about.
15. North American Association for Environmental Education, "The State of Climate Change Education: Findings from a National Survey of Educators," October 2022, https://eepro.naaee.org/learning/climate-change-education-what-are-we-hearing-educators-and-administrators.
16. Smithsonian Science Education Center, *Educating for Sustainable Development: Perspectives of U.S. and Global Educators Report,* 2023, https://ssec.si.edu/educating-for-sustainable-development-report.
17. Madeline Will, "U.S. Teachers Lag Behind Global Peers in Teaching About Sustainability. Here's Why," *Education Week,* September 5, 2023, https://www.edweek.org/teaching-learning/u-s-teachers-lag-behind-global-peers-in-teaching-about-sustainability-heres-why/2023/09.
18. Environmental and Climate Change Literacy Projects, https://www.ecclps.net/.

19. Madeline Will and Arianna Prothero, "Teens Know Climate Change Is Real. They Want Schools to Teach More About It," *Education Week*, November 21, 2022, https://www.edweek.org/teaching-learning/teens-know-climate-change-is-real-they-want-schools-to-teach-more-about-it/2022/11#.
20. Planet Media Aspen Institute and The Nature Conservancy, *Key Climate Principles (Appendix A)*, https://www.thisisplaneted.org/img/Key-Climate-Principles.pdf.
21. Los Angeles Board of Education, *Climate Literacy Resolution*, February 8, 2022, https://www.lausd.org/cms/lib/CA01000043/Centricity/Domain/1500/ClimateLiteracy016-2022.pdf.
22. *UDL Guidelines*, CAST, https://udlguidelines.cast.org/.
23. Owen L. Oliver and Center for Native American Youth, "Tribal Sovereignty Is Environmental Justice and Must Be Recognized by Schools," This Is Planet Ed, Aspen Institute, https://www.thisisplaneted.org/blog/tribal-sovereignty-is-environmental-justice.
24. New Harmony High School, https://newharmonyhigh.org/.
25. "A Letter from the Founding School Leader," About Us, New Harmony High School, https://newharmonyhigh.org/about-us/.
26. K12 Climate Action, *K12 Climate Action Plan*, Aspen Institute, September 2021, https://www.thisisplaneted.org/img/K12-ClimateActionPlan-Complete-Screen.pdf.
27. *UDL Guidelines*.
28. Jill Anderson, "What It Means to Learn Science," Harvard Graduate School of Education, December 3, 2020, https://www.gse.harvard.edu/ideas/edcast/20/12/what-it-means-learn-science.
29. Learning in Places Collaborative, http://learninginplaces.org/.
30. Learning in Places Collaborative, http://learninginplaces.org/.
31. K12 Climate Action, "Listening Session IV."
32. Anderson, "What It Means to Learn Science."
33. Laura E. Hernández et al., "Deeper Learning Networks: Taking Student-Centered Learning and Equity to Scale," *Learning Policy Institute*, October 21, 2019, https://learningpolicyinstitute.org/product/deeper-learning-networks-report.
34. Robert Pollin, Chirag Lala, and Shouvik Chakraborty, *Job Creation Estimates Through Proposed Inflation Reduction Act*, Political Economy Research Institute, University of Massachusetts Amherst, August 4, 2022, https://peri.umass.edu/publication/item/1633-job-creation-estimates-through-proposed-inflation-reduction-act.
35. "Transcript: Ezra Klein Interviews Bill McKibben," *The Ezra Klein Show*, *New York Times*, November 15, 2022, https://www.nytimes.com/2022/11/15/podcasts/transcript-ezra-klein-interviews-bill-mckibben.html.
36. Advance CTE, "Career Clusters," *Career Tech*, 2023, https://careertech.org/what-we-do/career-clusters/.

37. Nancy Lofholm, "Reimagining a Historic Granary as Hayden, Colorado Undergoes an Economic Reinvention," *CPR News*, October 18, 2023, https://www.cpr.org/2023/10/18/reimagining-a-historic-granary-as-hayden-colorado-undergoes-an-economic-reinvention/.
38. Hayden School District, *Strategic Plan*, https://drive.google.com/file/d/1JvtR-UbMgJ15JJwHQIFtJgcs_UirZONU/view.
39. Mark Jaffe, "Xcel Energy Moves Up Closure Dates for Coal-Fired Power Plant Near Steamboat Springs," *Colorado Sun*, January 4, 2021, https://coloradosun.com/2021/01/04/hayden-power-plant-early-closure-colorado/.
40. The Yampa Valley Partnership for Students, Stewardship, and Sustainability, https://www.yvps3.org/.
41. Lyra Colorado, "Building Climate Resiliency. Climatarium," https://www.lyracolorado.org/climatarium.
42. Ilona M. Otto et al., "Social Tipping Dynamics for Stabilizing Earth's Climate by 2050," *Proceedings of the National Academy of Sciences* 117, no. 5 (January 2020), https://doi.org/10.1073/pnas.190057711.

CHAPTER 4

1. National Weather Service, "Major Hurricane Maria—September 20, 2017," September 20, 2017, https://www.weather.gov/sju/maria2017.
2. Youth Development Institute of Puerto Rico and Estudios Técnicos, Inc., "The Impact of Hurricane Maria on Children in Puerto Rico," *ISSUU.com*, October 15, 2018, https://issuu.com/coleccionpuertorriquena/docs/instituto_juventud.
3. RAND Corporation, "Hurricanes Irma and Maria: Impact and Aftermath," *rand.org*, Homeland Security Operational Analysis Center, https://www.rand.org/hsrd/hsoac/projects/puerto-rico-recovery/hurricanes-irma-and-maria.html.
4. Youth Development Institute of Puerto Rico and Estudios Técnicos, Inc., "The Impact of Hurricane Maria on Children in Puerto Rico."
5. K12 Climate Action, "Listening Session III: How Can Schools Adapt to the Impacts of Climate Change?," This Is Planet Ed, Aspen Institute, https://www.thisisplaneted.org/blog/listening-session-iii-schools-adapt-to-climate-change-1.
6. Institute for Education Sciences, "Table 203.20: Enrollment in Public Elementary and Secondary Schools by Region, State, and Jurisdiction: Selected Years, Fall 1990 through Fall 2031," National Center for Education Statistics, https://nces.ed.gov/programs/digest/d22/tables/dt22_203.20.asp.
7. Dánica Coto, "Officials Detail Hurricane Fiona Damage to Puerto Rico Grid," Associated Press, September 29, 2022, https://apnews.com/article/hurricanes-caribbean-storms-power-outages-puerto-rico-5d54ac54f0cc1b69c3c2294a4638d9db.
8. Kavitha Cardoza, "In the 6th-Largest U.S. District, Natural Disasters Have Disrupted Schooling for Years," *All Things Considered, NPR*, August 17, 2023, https://www.npr.org/2023/08/16/1193722562/puerto-rico-schools-education.

9. Kavitha Cardoza, "Are the Challenges of Puerto Rico's Schools a Taste of What Other Districts Will Face?," *Hechinger Report*, April 3, 2023, https://hechingerreport.org/are-the-challenges-of-puerto-ricos-schools-a-taste-of-what-other-districts-will-face/.
10. United Nations, "Climate Adaptation," https://www.un.org/en/climatechange/climate-adaptation.
11. National Oceanic and Atmospheric Administration (NOAA), "The World Just Sweltered Through Its Hottest August on Record," September 14, 2023, https://www.noaa.gov/news/world-just-sweltered-through-its-hottest-august-on-record.
12. Eric Roston, "As School Started in the U.S., So Did the School Closures for Heat," *Time*, September 9, 2023, https://time.com/6312416/as-school-started-in-the-u-s-so-did-the-school-closures-for-heat/.
13. Laura Schifter, "Opinion: How I Talk to My Kids About Climate Change," *CNN*, June 10, 2023, https://www.cnn.com/2023/06/09/opinions/east-cost-smog-climate-change-action-education-schifter/index.html.
14. Troy Closson, "More Than 150 New York School Buildings Flooded, and One Had to Evacuate," *New York Times*, September 29, 2023, https://www.nytimes.com/2023/09/29/nyregion/nyc-schools-flooding.html.
15. National Aeronautics and Space Administration, "The Effects of Climate Change," August 9, 2021, https://climate.nasa.gov/effects/.
16. National Oceanic and Atmospheric Administration (NOAA), "U. S. Struck with Historic Number of Billion-Dollar Disasters in 2023," January 9, 2024, https://www.noaa.gov/news/us-struck-with-historic-number-of-billion-dollar-disasters-in-2023.
17. Probable Futures is a nonprofit climate literacy initiative that makes tools, stories, and resources available to everyone, everywhere, at https://probablefutures.org/.
18. Maanvi Singh, "American Football Season Is Getting Hotter. Young Players Are Dying," *Guardian*, September 24, 2023, https://www.theguardian.com/world/2023/sep/24/football-player-heat-deaths-athlete.
19. Center for Climate Integrity (CCI), *Hotter Days, Higher Costs: The Cooling Crisis in America's Classrooms*, Center for Climate Integrity, September 2021, https://coolingcrisis.org/uploads/media/HotterDaysHigherCosts-CCI-September2021.pdf.
20. Baltimore City Public Schools, "Schools without AC," https://www.baltimorecityschools.org/o/bcps/page/ac.
21. Probable Futures, Maps of Temperature: Days Above 32°C (90°F), https://probablefutures.org/maps/?volume=heat&selected_map=days_above_32c&map_version=latest&warming_scenario=0.5&map_projection=mercator#10/39.3201/-76.6006.

22. Between 1971 and 2000, the average surface temperature of the Earth was 0.5°C above preindustrial levels. In that same time period, Baltimore experienced an average of twenty-two days above 90°F.
23. US Climate Resilience Toolkit, "Assess Vulnerability and Risk," updated May 10, 2024, https://toolkit.climate.gov/steps-to-resilience/assess-vulnerability-risk.
24. US Climate Resilience Toolkit, "Assess Vulnerability and Risk."
25. Julia Busiek, "Hot Spots," Trust for Public Land, https://www.tpl.org/stories/hot-spots.
26. Jonathan Klein, "Opinion: With Schools, Pay Less Now or Pay More Later," *The Hill*, July 20, 2021, https://thehill.com/opinion/energy-environment/563936-with-schools-pay-less-now-or-pay-more-later/.
27. Caroline Preston, "Coronavirus Is the Practice Run for Schools but Soon Comes Climate Change," May 23, 2020, *Hechinger Report*, https://hechingerreport.org/coronavirus-is-the-practice-run-for-schools-but-soon-comes-climate-change/.
28. K12 Climate Action, "Listening Session III."
29. Centers for Disease Control and Prevention (CDC), "Helping Children Cope with Emergencies," Caring for Children in a Disaster, reviewed September 1, 2020, https://www.cdc.gov/childrenindisasters/helping-children-cope.html.
30. Caroline Hickman et al., "Climate Anxiety in Children and Young People and Their Beliefs About Government Responses to Climate Change: A Global Survey," *Lancet* 5, no. 12 (December 2021), https://www.thelancet.com/journals/lanplh/article/PIIS2542-5196(21)00278-3/fulltext#seccestitle130.
31. Melody Schreiber, "Addressing Climate Change Concerns in Practice," *Monitor on Psychology* 52, no. 2 (March 2021): 30, https://www.apa.org/monitor/2021/03/ce-climate-change.
32. National Child Traumatic Stress Network, Schools Committee, *Creating, Supporting, and Sustaining Trauma-Informed Schools: A System Framework* (Los Angeles, CA: National Center for Child Traumatic Stress, 2017), https://www.nctsn.org/sites/default/files/resources//creating_supporting_sustaining_trauma_informed_schools_a_systems_framework.pdf.
33. K12 Climate Action, "Listening Session III."
34. Karen Diegmueller, "Nearly 3 Weeks After Hurricane, Dade Schools Are Set to Open," *Education Week*, September 16, 1992, https://www.edweek.org/education/nearly-3-weeks-after-hurricane-dade-schools-set-to-open/1992/09#.
35. Melissa Feito, "Hurricane Andrew Changed Preparedness Forever," *NPR*, August 30, 2022, https://www.wusf.org/weather/2022-08-30/hurricane-andrew-changed-preparedness-forever.
36. Preston, "Coronavirus Is the Practice Run for Schools."
37. Miami-Dade County, "Miami-Dade County Mayor Levine Cava Releases Climate Action Strategy Progress Report on Earth Day," press release, April

24, 2023, https://www.miamidade.gov/global/release.page?Mduid_release=rel1682338378079720#.
38. K12 Climate Action, "Listening Session III."
39. A. J. Hat et al., "Overview: Understanding Risks, Impacts, and Responses," in *Fifth National Climate Assessment*, ed. Allison Crimmins et al. (Washington, DC: US Global Change Research Program, 2023), 1-1–1-47, https://nca2023.globalchange.gov/downloads/NCA5_Ch1_Overview.pdf.
40. Kate Payne, "'I See Myself in These Students': 20,000 Immigrant Children Join Miami-Dade Schools," *NPR*, May 24, 2023, https://www.wlrn.org/education/2023-05-24/miami-dade-schools-immigrant-students.
41. UN Environment Programme, "Helping Farmers Beat the Climate Crisis in Central America's Dry Corridor," June 16, 2023, https://www.unep.org/news-and-stories/story/helping-farmers-beat-climate-crisis-central-americas-dry-corridor.
42. Kate Payne, "Miami-Dade Schools Welcome Migrant Students—but Enrollment Surge Strains Staffing and Mental Health Services," *NPR*, January 20, 2023, https://www.wlrn.org/education/2023-01-20/miami-dade-schools-welcome-migrant-students-with-open-arms-but-surge-strains-staffing-and-mental-health-services.
43. K12 Climate Action, "Listening Session III."
44. Space to Grow, "Our Model," Space to Grow Greening Chicago, Healthy Schools Campaign and Openlands, 2022, https://www.spacetogrowchicago.org/about/our-model/.
45. Santa Barbara United School District, *LCFF Budget Overview for Parents*, School Year 2022–23, https://resources.finalsite.net/images/v1668602572/sbunifiedorg/uipoqewlxtdt7khuk8hh/21-22SantaBarbaraUSDLCAP.pdf.
46. Cal Fire, "Thomas Fire," *CA.gov*, https://www.fire.ca.gov/incidents/2017/12/4/thomas-fire/.
47. US Geological Survey, "What Should I Know About Wildfires and Debris Flows?," https://www.usgs.gov/faqs/what-should-i-know-about-wildfires-and-debris-flows.
48. Generation180, "California School District Responds to Climate Emergency with Energy Resilience," September 26, 2022, https://generation180.org/blog/california-school-district-responds-to-climate-emergency-with-energy-resilience/.
49. Generation180, "California School District Responds to Climate Emergency."

CHAPTER 5

1. Solar Energy Industries Association (SEIA), "Net Metering," (Washington, DC: SEIA, n.d.), https://www.seia.org/initiatives/net-metering.
2. K12 Climate Action, "K12 Climate Action Plan 2021," This Is Planet Ed, Aspen Institute, https://www.thisisplaneted.org/blog/climate-action-plan-2021.

3. New Buildings Institute (NBI), "Decarbonization Roadmap Guide for School Building Decision Makers," April 25, 2022, https://newbuildings.org/resource/decarbonization-roadmap-guide-for-school-building-decision-makers/.
4. Erika Eitland, Lacey Klingensmith, Piers MacNaughton, Jose Cedeno Laurent, Jack Spengler, Ari Bernstein, and Joseph G. Allen, *Foundations for Student Success: How School Buildings Influence Student Health, Thinking, and Performance*, Harvard T. H. Chan School of Public Health, https://schools.forhealth.org/wp-content/uploads/2020/02/Schools_ForHealth_UpdatedJan21.pdf.
5. Emma Hines and Sara Ross, *HVAC Choices for Student Health and Learning*, UndauntedK12 & RMI, 2023, https://www.undauntedk12.org/hvac-rmi.
6. "Asthma," Harvard T. H. Chan School of Public Health, https://www.hsph.harvard.edu/c-change/subtopics/climate-change-and-asthma/; United States Environmental Protection Agency (EPA), "Why Indoor Air Quality Is Important to Schools," https://www.epa.gov/iaq-schools/why-indoor-air-quality-important-schools.
7. Pew Charitable Trusts, "Healthy School Lunches Improve Kids' Habits," December 1, 2015, https://www.pewtrusts.org/en/research-and-analysis/articles/2015/12/01/healthy-school-lunches-improve-kids-habits?_ga=1.106870659.1690432487.1439834032.
8. K12 Climate Action, "Building for the Future: Investing in Climate Change Mitigation and Adaptation in Schools: Day 1," This Is Planet Ed, Aspen Institute, https://www.thisisplaneted.org/blog/building-for-the-future-day-1.
9. City of Boston, "A Green New Deal for Boston Public Schools," updated July 31, 2024, https://www.boston.gov/education/green-new-deal-boston-public-schools; City of New York, "NYC Schools Leading the Charge," 2024, https://www.nyc.gov/content/getstuffdone/pages/electric-schools.
10. K12 Climate Action and World Resources Institute, "Education and Climate Provisions in the Infrastructure Investment and Jobs Act," This Is Planet Ed, Aspen Institute, https://www.thisisplaneted.org/blog/education-and-climate-iija.
11. United States Environmental Protection Agency (EPA), "Biden-Harris Administration Will Double Clean School Bus Rebate Awards to Nearly $1 Billion," September 29, 2022, updated September 11, 2023, https://www.epa.gov/newsreleases/biden-harris-administration-will-double-clean-school-bus-rebate-awards-nearly-1.
12. This Is Planet Ed and World Resources Institute, "K12 Education and Climate Provisions in the Inflation Reduction Act," This Is Planet Ed, Aspen Institute, https://www.thisisplaneted.org/blog/school-climate-provisions-in-the-inflation-reduction-act.
13. United States Environmental Protection Agency (EPA), "Scope 1 and Scope 2 Inventory Guidance," updated March 8, 2024, https://www.epa.gov/climateleadership/scope-1-and-scope-2-inventory-guidance.

14. AFTHQ and K12 Climate Action, "Back to School for All Tour Highlights Net-Zero School Building," *YouTube*, https://www.youtube.com/watch?v=-W5vhOq6gFY.
15. United States Environmental Protection Agency (EPA), "Inventory of U.S. Greenhouse Gas Emissions and Sinks," updated April 11, 2024, https://www.epa.gov/ghgemissions/inventory-us-greenhouse-gas-emissions-and-sinks.
16. 21st Century School Fund, Inc.; International WELL Building Institute; and National Council on School Facilities, *2021 State of Our Schools: America's PK–12 Public School Facilities*, 2021, https://static1.squarespace.com/static/5a5ccab5bff20008734885eb/t/618aab5d79d53d3ef439097c/1636477824193/SOOS-IWBI2021-2_21CSF+print_final.pdf.
17. American Society of Civil Engineers (ASCE), "2021 Report Card for America's Infrastructure: Schools," ASCE's 2021 Infrastructure Report Card, https://infrastructurereportcard.org/cat-item/schools-infrastructure/.
18. US Government Accountability Office, *K–12 Education: School Districts Frequently Identified Multiple Building Systems Needing Updates or Replacement*, June 4, 2020, https://www.gao.gov/products/gao-20-494?source=ra.
19. Mary Filardo, Jeffrey M. Vincent, and Kevin J. Sullivan, "How Crumbling School Facilities Perpetuate Inequality," *Kappan*, April 29, 2019, https://kappanonline.org/how-crumbling-school-facilities-perpetuate-inequality-filardo-vincent-sullivan/.
20. United States Environmental Protection Agency (EPA), *Energy Efficiency Programs in K–12 Schools: A Guide to Developing and Implementing Greenhouse Gas Reduction Programs, Local Government Climate and Energy Strategy Series*, 2011, https://www.epa.gov/sites/default/files/2015-08/documents/k-12_guide.pdf.
21. Hannah Hall and Eric Nielsen, "How Do Children Spend Their Time? Time Use and Skill Development in the PSID," Board of Governors of the Federal Reserve System, FEDS Notes, May 26, 2020, https://www.federalreserve.gov/econres/notes/feds-notes/how-do-children-spend-their-time-time-use-and-skill-development-in-the-psid-20200526.html.
22. Office of Energy Efficiency & Renewable Energy, "A Common Definition for Zero Energy Buildings," *Energy.gov*, https://www.energy.gov/eere/buildings/articles/common-definition-zero-energy-buildings.
23. Paul A. Torcellini, Nathaniel Allen, and Maureen McIntyre, "Plowing Through the Cost Barrier: Zero Energy K–12 Schools for Less: Preprint" (Golden, CO: National Renewable Energy Laboratory, 2020), NREL/CP-5500-77414, https://www.nrel.gov/docs/fy20osti/77414.pdf.
24. New Buildings Institute (NBI), *2019 Zero Energy Schools Watchlist*, 2019, https://newbuildings.org/wp-content/uploads/2019/02/2019_SchoolsWatchlist.pdf.
25. Arlington (VA) Public Schools, "APS Strategic Plan 2022–28," https://www.apsva.us/strategic-plan/.
26. AFTHQ and K12 Climate Action, "Back to School for All Tour."
27. Hines and Ross, *HVAC Choices for Student Health & Learning*.

28. Berkeley County Board of Education, Martinsburg, West Virginia, "Case Study: Performance Contracting," CMTA, Inc., 2024, https://www.cmta.com/results/case-studies/berkeley-county-schools.
29. Generation180, *Brighter Future: A Study on Solar in U.S. K–12 Schools,* 4th ed. (Charlottesville, VA: Genration180, September 2022), https://generation180.org/resource/brighter-future-a-study-on-solar-in-us-k-12-schools-2022/.
30. Batesville (AR) School District (BSD), "BSD Solar Initiative," https://www.batesvilleschools.com/domain/176.
31. Generation180, "Batesville, AR: Energy Savings Reap Investments in Teacher Pay and Education," September 14, 2020, https://generation180.org/batesville-ar-energy-savings-reap-investments-in-teacher-pay-and-education/.
32. United States Environmental Protection Agency (EPA), "Sources of Greenhouse Gas Emissions," updated June 5, 2024, https://www.epa.gov/ghgemissions/sources-greenhouse-gas-emissions.
33. Sydney Page, "These Kids Ride a 'Bike Bus' to School," *Washington Post,* October 11, 2022, https://www.washingtonpost.com/lifestyle/2022/10/11/bike-bus-school-sam-balto/.
34. School Bus Fleet, "Fact Book 2021: Pupil Transportation Statistics: School Transportation 2018–19 School Year," 2021, https://www.schoolbusfleet.com/download?id=10131920&dl=.1.
35. Phillip Burgoyne-Allen, Katrina Boone, Juliet Squire, and Jennifer O'Neal Schiess, "The Challenges and Opportunities in School Transportation Today," *Bellwether,* July 23, 2018, https://bellwether.org/publications/challenges-and-opportunities-school-transportation-today/.
36. Electric School Bus Initiative, "Why We Need to Transition to Electric School Buses," October 17, 2022, https://electricschoolbusinitiative.org/why-we-need-transition-electric-school-buses.
37. Wes Austin, Garth Heutel, and Daniel Kreisman, "School Bus Emissions, Student Health, and Academic Performance," National Bureau of Economic Research, Cambridge, MA, Working Paper No. 25641, March 2019, https://www.nber.org/system/files/working_papers/w25641/w25641.pdf.
38. Electric School Bus Initiative, "Why We Need to Transition to Electric School Buses."
39. Norrice M. Liu and Jonathan Grigg, "Diesel, Children and Respiratory Disease," *BMJ Paediatrics Open* 2, no. 1 (2019), https://www.ncbi.nlm.nih.gov/pmc/articles/PMC5976105/#R4.
40. Matt Casale and Brendan Mahoney, *Paying for Electric Buses,* US PIRG Education Fund, Fall 2018, https://publicinterestnetwork.org/wp-content/uploads/2018/10/National-Paying-for-Electric-Buses-1.pdf.
41. Highland Electric Fleets, "MCPS Celebrates Largest School Bus Electrification Project in the United States," *PRN Newswire,* October 25, 2022, https://www.prnewswire.com/news-releases/mcps-celebrates-largest-school-bus-electrification-project-in-the-united-states-301658940.html.

42. School Nutrition Association, "School Meal Statistics," https://schoolnutrition.org/about-school-meals/school-meal-statistics/#2.
43. Kids' Safe and Healthful Foods Project, *School Meal Programs Innovate to Improve Student Nutrition,* Pew Charitable Trusts and Robert Wood Johnson Foundation, December 2016, https://www.pewtrusts.org/~/media/assets/2016/12/school_meal_programs_innovate_to_improve_student_nutrition.pdf.
44. Gail Woodward-Lopez et al., "Is Scratch-Cooking a Cost-Effective Way to Prepare Healthy School Meals with US Department of Agriculture Foods?," *Journal of the Academy of Nutrition and Dietetics* 114, no. 9 (July 2014), https://www.jandonline.org/article/S2212-2672(14)00498-5/abstract.
45. K12 Climate Action, "Food: What Is School Food?," K12 Climate Action, The Aspen Institute, https://www.thisisplaneted.org/img/K12-SPL20-FOOD-Screen.pdf.
46. Jaimie N. Davis et al., "School-Based Gardening, Cooking and Nutrition Intervention Increased Vegetable Intake but Did Not Reduce BMI: Texas Sprouts: A Cluster Randomized Controlled Trial," *International Journal of Behavioral Nutrition and Physical Activity* 16, no 18 (2021), https://ijbnpa.biomedcentral.com/articles/10.1186/s12966-021-01087-x.
47. Office of the State Superintendent of Education (OSSE), "School Gardens Program (SGP)," *DC.gov,* https://osse.dc.gov/service/school-gardens-program-sgp.
48. World Wildlife Fund (WWF), *Food Waste Warriors: A Deep Dive into Food Waste in US Schools,* 2019, https://c402277.ssl.cf1.rackcdn.com/publications/1271/files/original/FoodWasteWarriorR_CS_121819.pdf?1576689275.
49. Juliana F. W. Cohen, Scott Richardson, S. Bryn Austin, Christina D. Economos, and Eric B. Rimm, "School Lunch Waste Among Middle School Students: Implications for Nutrients Consumed and Food Waste Costs," *American Journal of Preventive Medicine* 44, no. 2 (February 2013), https://www.ncbi.nlm.nih.gov/pmc/articles/PMC3788640/.
50. San Diego Unified School District (SDUSD), "Love Food Not Waste Project Summary 2022–23," SDUSD Sustainability, August 4, 2022, https://www.sdusd-sustainability.com/_files/ugd/486c25_abda1dee36814ddea35c45afe890a3a1.pdf.

CHAPTER 6

1. Ballotpedia, "Shiva Rajbhandari," https://ballotpedia.org/Shiva_Rajbhandari.
2. Fortesa Latifi, "Shiva Rajbhandari, Idaho Teen Activist, Won Election to the Boise School Board," Politics, *Teen Vogue,* September 16, 2022, https://www.teenvogue.com/story/shiva-rajbhandari-school-board.
3. Boise School District, "Sustainability Update & Clean Energy Commitment—Action Item," Board of Trustees Meeting, November 8, 2021, https://simbli.eboardsolutions.com/SB_Meetings/ViewMeeting.aspx?S=36030877&MID=834&Tab=Agenda&enIID=QvEGhtslshVvhTbGgP9iABIslshA%3D%3D.

4. Kaylee Domzalski, "How a High School Student Became a School Board Member," *Education Week*, October 18, 2022, https://www.edweek.org/leadership/video-how-a-high-school-student-became-a-school-board-member/2022/10.
5. C40 Cities Climate Leadership Group and C40 Knowledge Hub, "Implementation Guided: How to Get Started on Your City's Climate Action Plan," https://www.c40knowledgehub.org/s/guide-navigation?language=en_US&guideRecordId=a3t1Q0000007lEWQAY&guideArticleRecordId=a3s1Q000001iahmQAA.
6. Lauren Simmons, Michelle Faggert, Laura Schifter, and Medha Iyer, *Education Uncapped: The Potential of the Education Sector in City Climate Action Planning,* This Is Planet Ed, Aspen Institute, 2023, https://www.thisisplaneted.org/img/PlanetED-EducationUncapped-Screen-1.pdf.
7. Dallas Independent School District, "Environment & Climate Action Resolution for Dallas ISD Spring 2020," February 27, 2020, https://go.boarddocs.com/tx/disd/Board.nsf/files/BLHUJV7C473D/$file/DISD%20Climate%20Resolution%20FINAL%2002%2027%202020pdf.doc%20(002).pdf.
8. Michelle Aslam, "Dallas Teens Push for Local Actions on Climate Change," *Dallas Morning News,* April 10, 2020, https://www.dallasnews.com/news/education/2020/04/10/dallas-teens-push-for-local-actions-on-climate-change/.
9. Public Education Leadership Project (PELP), "Coherence Framework," Harvard University, https://pelp.fas.harvard.edu/coherence-framework.
10. Salt Lake City School District, "District Demographics," https://www.slcschools.org/schools/district-demographics.
11. Salt Lake City School District, *2040 Sustainability Action Plan: Sustainability, Clean Energy, and Carbon Neutrality,* September 2021, https://resources.finalsite.net/images/v1641931356/slcschoolsorg/irjphywgl0dtrb8n8in0/sustainability-resolution-english.pdf.
12. Peter O'Dowd, "Collapse of Utah's Great Salt Lake Is 'So Close You Can Feel It,'" WBUR, November 7, 2023, https://www.wbur.org/hereandnow/2023/11/07/great-salt-lake-utah-crisis.
13. Isabella Gomez and Saeed Ahmed, "How a Group of Teenagers Convinced the Utah Legislature to Recognize Climate Change," *CNN Health*, May 22, 2018, https://www.cnn.com/2018/05/22/health/utah-students-climate-change-trnd/index.html.
14. Salt Lake City School District Board of Education, "Resolution to Establish Goals for Sustainability, Clean Energy, and Carbon Neutrality," June 2, 2020, https://resources.finalsite.net/images/v1643733492/slcschoolsorg/rcw3qlhqvpk1hk0lypoj/SignedSustainabilityResolution.pdf.
15. Salt Lake City School District, *2040 Sustainability Action Plan.*
16. Salt Lake City School District, "Sustainability in Action," https://resources.finalsite.net/images/v1665592197/slcschoolsorg/lywp0efwlzc4gilhl3ud/PerformanceContractInformationSheet295Million.pdf.

17. Denver Public Schools, *DPS Climate Action Plan 2023, Issuu,* December 19, 2022, https://issuu.com/dpscommunications/docs/dps_climate_action_plan_pages.
18. Arianna Prothero, "Leader to Learn From: This Leader Partners with Students to Build a More Sustainable Future for Her District," *Education Week,* February 5, 2024, https://www.edweek.org/leaders/2024/this-leader-partners-with-students-to-build-a-more-sustainable-future-for-her-district.
19. Deb Kinder, "Life & Culture: Flood in 1977 Was Third to Devastate Johnstown," *Penn Live Patriot-News,* July 19, 2019, https://www.pennlive.com/life/2019/07/flood-in-1977-was-third-to-devastate-johnstown.html.
20. Prince George's County (MD) Public Schools (PGCPS), "Facts and Figures," September 30, 2022, https://www.pgcps.org/facts-and-figures/.
21. Prince George's County (MD) Public Schools (PGCPS), "About PGCPS," https://www.pgcps.org/about-pgcps.
22. PGCPS Board of Education Climate Change Action Plan Focus Work Group, *Climate Change Action Plan (CCAP) Priority Recommendations,* April 28, 2022, *Google,* https://drive.google.com/file/d/1eS5YuvflbLyDsnw5QWwqlTltKBeEjx28/view.

CHAPTER 7

1. Quote Investigator, "Never Doubt That a Small Group of Thoughtful, Committed Citizens Can Change the World; Indeed, It's the Only Thing That Ever Has," November 12, 2017, https://quoteinvestigator.com/2017/11/12/change-world/#google_vignette.
2. Prince George's County (MD) Public Schools (PGCPS), "Climate Change Action Plan (CCAP)," 2024, https://www.pgcps.org/about-pgcps/climate-change-action-plan.
3. Denver Public Schools (DPS), "Explore DPS Climate Action," https://sustainability.dpsk12.org/.
4. The Santa Fe Institute is a research organization dedicated to the study of complex systems, including complexity theory. Its website (https://www.santafe.edu/what-is-complex-systems-science) offers a wealth of resources, including research papers, articles, and information about ongoing projects related to complexity theory.
5. Frances Westley, Brenda Zimmerman, and Michael Quinn Patton, *Getting to Maybe: How the World Is Changed* (Toronto: Penguin Random House Canada, 2007).
6. Everett Rogers, *Diffusion of Innovations,* 5th ed. (New York: Free Press, 2003).
7. Generation180, *Brighter Future: A Study on Solar in U.S. K–12 Schools,* 4th ed. (Charlottesville, VA: Genration180, September 2022), https://generation180.org/resource/brighter-future-a-study-on-solar-in-us-k-12-schools-2022/.

8. RMI and UndauntedK12, *HVAC Choices for Student Health and Learning: What Policymakers, School Leaders, and Advocates Need to Know,* January 2023, https://www.undauntedk12.org/hvac-rmi.
9. Sam Kaner, *Facilitator's Guide to Participatory Decision-Making,* 2nd ed. (San Francisco: Jossey-Bass, 2007). This book is an indispensable resource for facilitating conversations, planning and leading meetings, and supporting effective multi-stakeholder collaborations.
10. The work of Dr. Marshall Ganz of Harvard University has deeply shaped the field of community organizing. See Dogwood Initiative, Leadnow, One Cowichan, the David Suzuki Foundation, Stonehouse Institute, and genius, *Organizing: People, Power, Change,* https://leadingchangenetwork.org/wp-content/uploads/2021/08/Organizers_Handbook.pdf, for a succinct presentation of Ganz's organizing models and principles.
11. We recommend Becky Bond and Zack Exley, *Rules for Revolutions: How Organizing Can Change Everything* (White River Junction, VT: Chelsea Green, 2016), for practical insights on leveraging organizing practices within campaigns.
12. Stephanie K. Barr, Jennifer E. Cross, and Brian H. Dunbar, *The Whole-School Sustainability Framework: Guiding Principles for Integrating Sustainability into All Aspects of a School Organization* (Washington, DC: Center for Green Schools, 2014), https://centerforgreenschools.org/sites/default/files/resource-files/Whole-School_Sustainability_Framework.pdf, offers districts an opportunity to see sustainability at the center of schools' work across organizational culture, physical place, and educational programing. Green Schools National Network, *GreenPrint™: A Framework for Becoming a Healthy, Equitable, and Sustainable School,* October 2021, https://greenschoolsnationalnetwork.org/wp-content/uploads/2023/01/GreenPrint%E2%84%A2-2023-1.pdf, centers health, equity, and sustainability highlighting opportunities to integrate these pillars across school leadership, culture, facilities, and curriculum.
13. For example, the New Buildings Institute (NBI) (https://newbuildings.org/resource/decarbonization-roadmap-guide-for-school-building-decision-makers/) released a new *Decarbonization Roadmap Guide for School Building Decision Makers* in April 2022 for those "interested in healthy, efficient, carbon neutral school design, construction, and operation." Green Schoolyards America (https://www.greenschoolyards.org/forest-resource-library) manages a free, growing online library filled with practical resources to support schools and school districts as they plan, develop, use, and manage schoolyard forests.
14. Katharine Hayhoe, "In the Face of Climate Change, We Must Act So That We Can Feel Hopeful—Not the Other Way Around," *Time,* August 12, 2021, https://time.com/6089999/climate-change-hope/.

ACKNOWLEDGMENTS

WE ARE SO grateful to the many people who embraced our climate journeys, supported us through launching new initiatives, continue to build momentum for action, and work hard every day to make a difference. We would especially like to thank the individuals profiled in this book for their leadership in schools, communities, and states and around the country. Their willingness to be part of this project will help more students, parents, educators, and education leaders know what they can do to make a difference. We also want to thank the people who are leading efforts and organizations at the intersection of climate change and education. Their enthusiasm for working collaboratively and their persistence has already had and will continue to have a lasting impact on students, schools, and our future.

FROM LAURA

I would particularly like to thank the people who extended their time, energy, support, and relationships to help me turn something from a concept note in a Google document to an initiative impacting education across the country. Thank you to Roberto Rodriguez; Kyle Lierman; Shira Miller; my former Hill colleagues Jamie Fasteau, Denise Forte, Ruth Friedman, Kara Marchione, MaryEllen McGuire, Livia Lam, Charmaine

Mercer, Melissa Luce, Michael Yudin, and Emma Vadehra; and Michael Madnick, whose strategy, insights, and introductions in my earliest efforts helped shape the foundation for K12 Climate Action. Thank you to Ellen Pinschmidt, Gardiner Lapham, Katherine Lucas, Sam Mason, and Chris Bolger for helping me understand what it means to take action at a school level while supporting my efforts to build a broader vision for education as well. I would also like to extend my gratitude to the many people I spoke with along the way, whose feedback helped make this work more impactful. Thank you to Greg Gershuny and Nikki DeVignes for helping me create a home within the Aspen Institute.

I am so tremendously grateful to John B. King Jr. and Christine Todd Whitman for their steady leadership, collaborative perspective, positive attitude, and ability to get stuff done. Thank you especially to John for not only going above and beyond in maximizing the work's potential as cochair but also modeling leadership at the intersection of climate and education now as chancellor of the State University of New York. I am also thankful to all the K12 Climate Action commissioners—Naina Agrawal-Hardin, Megan Bang, Vic Barrett, Carlos Curbelo, Linda Darling-Hammond, Debra Duardo, Lisa Hoyos, Richard Knoeppel, Dan Lashof, Jack Markell, Pedro Martinez, Marc Morial, Janet Murguía, Kiera O'Brien, Becky Pringle, Carla Thompson Payton, Pedro Rivera, Valerie Rockefeller, Nikki Santos, and Randi Weingarten—for developing this collective vision for schools, the speakers who presented before the commission, and to Emily Katz, Mykelle Richburg, Nell Callahan, Philippa Martinez-Berrier, and Michelle Faggert for supporting the efforts behind the action plan.

I would also like to acknowledge Chi Kim, Mary Seawell, Kate Jaffe, Clarke Williams, María Ortiz Pérez, and Frank Gettridge for their friendship, encouragement, and willingness to be a sounding board throughout this work. Dean Bridget Terry Long, thank you for recognizing the tremendous impact of climate change on our education system and the need for the Harvard Graduate School of Education to help prepare education leaders for success in a changing climate. Thank you to Erin

Beaumont and Greta Williams for always being there for me and helping me create space to finish this book.

A huge thank you to Jonathan Klein for your leadership, partnership on this project, and our alliance moving this work forward together.

As our efforts have continued to expand to This Is Planet Ed, I am so grateful for the time and commitment from leaders and partners on our Higher Ed Climate Action Task Force, Planet Media Task Force, and Early Years Climate Action Task Force, especially our cochairs Millie García, Kim Hunter Reed, Gary Knell, Katharine Hayhoe, Diana Rauner, and Antwanye Ford, and for support and partnership from Terri Taylor, Kim O'Dell, Katie Cutler, Felicia DeHaney, Jon-Paul Bianchi, Bill Moses, and Lois DeBacker. I'm also thankful for the work and support from the broader This Is Planet Ed team Sophia Powless, Sarah Robbins, Lauren Simmons, Anya Kamenetz, Rory O'Sullivan, Ajoy Vase, and the team at Kemerling Design.

I owe a huge debt of gratitude to the late Tom Hehir, my friend, teacher, mentor, and promoter, who taught me I could be an author and a proud dyslexic.

Finally, I would like to thank my family, Matt Scriven and Rick and Jenni Schifter, and my sisters Rachel, Danni, and Cassie, for believing in me, caring for the kids, answering my calls, and putting up with me through this work. And of course, a huge thank you to my daughters, Ellie, Issie, and Thea, who fill my life with joy, curiosity, inspiration, dancing, and love.

FROM JONATHAN

Beginnings matter and dozens of leaders spent time with me as I worked to understand the intersection of educational equity and climate change. Thanks to each of them. Significant in this process were Sara Ross and Jennifer Moses, who were with me through countless conversations and started the Undaunted ball rolling.

Since my pivot to climate in 2020, my work has been a joyful, almost daily collaboration with Sara Ross. Sara and I collaborated for nearly a year during the COVID-19 pandemic before finally meeting in person. Our partnership, defined by our complementarity, trust, humor, and ambition, has been the driving force behind this incredible Undaunted journey. Thank you, Sara, for continually saying yes and for bringing your unwavering commitment and smarts to our shared vision.

Leadership is a team sport, and I'm grateful for the dedication and determination of my teammates and collaborators within Undaunted-land: Sarah Heine, Stephanie Seidmon, Skye Fournier, Justin Barra, Ken Doane, Jack Holzman, Josune Menendez, Amy Omand, Ruth Richerson, Greg Nelson, Jonathan Schorr, Brenda Casselius, Emma Bloomberg, Sage Welch, Chloe Zilliac, Matt Hammer, Kristen Hengtgen, interns and fellows, and the teams at BeClear and Sunstone Strategies. Special thanks to Ken for his insightful comments, suggestions, and feedback on early draft sections of this book.

My gratitude goes as well to the many generous supporters and funders who make Undaunted's work possible. Special thanks to Bob Spencer, Jennifer Moses and Ron Beller, Jackie Hindawi, Mara and Rick Wallace, David Sweet, Larry Kramer, Carrie Doyle, Abbey Banks, Andy Karetsky, Shanti Kleiman, Swati Mylavarapu, Matt Rogers, Keely Anson, Caroline Dillon, Ning Mosberger-Tang, Greg Rock, Kate Goss, Steve Toben, Antha Williams, Kelly Schultz, Sierra Martinez, Jessica Tritsch, Jess Lubetsky, Anu Cairo, Anne Marie Burgoyne, Daniel Reyes, Colin Liu, and the Emerson Collective Fellows team. Many of you took early risks to invest in me and our team when Undaunted was barely more than a Google doc and some PowerPoint slides. Your sustained generosity is powering Undaunted into the future.

Thank you to Christina Heitz, Talia Kolasinski, and John Deasy for supporting me and giving Undaunted its first home at Cambiar Education. Thanks to Alex Johnston for the invitation to participate in Joyful Impact and for more than a decade of coaching and wise counsel.

So many individuals and collaborators have generously welcomed me into this community and shared their expertise with passion and patience. Thank you: Lisa Patel, Jeff Vincent, Reilly Loveland, Leah Stokes, Merrian Borgeson, Jose Torres, David Weiskopf, Tiffany Mok, Julia Sebastian, Sharon Danks, Kirk Ann Taylor, Rick Brown, Alvin Lee, Mary Perry, Jody London, Joel Rosenberg, Serena Campas, Mary Ann Dewan, Sarah Ranney, David Boundy, Ted Tiffany, Karin Goldmark, Anthony deGuzman, Brian Turner, Michael Downs, and John King. I'm so proud to be in this work with you.

Thanks to my partners at Ten Strands—Andra Yeghoian, Karen Cowe, Jilliann M'Barki, and Will Parish—for bringing your powerful networks and knowledge built over decades to our California work. I value your friendship, partnership, and expertise.

I am deeply grateful to Laura Schifter for her leadership in our field and for her invitation to collaborate on this project. Laura's vision and persistence saw this through to the finish line.

Many longtime collaborators on my education journey encouraged my exploration of this intersection and have been willing to come with me and support this work. Thanks to Mike Buman, Brian Stanley, Wendy Kopp, Jonathan Travers, Jonas Chartock, Jeff Kutash, Jessica Stewart, Hae-Sin Thomas, and Brian Rogers. I am also grateful to my Oakland education and GO Public Schools team, boards, and community for decades of shared effort and aspiration. I carry lessons and inspiration from our work together into this new chapter.

I could not do this work without the steadfast support of my family and friends here in Oakland, California, and around the country. I will be fifty years old when this book is published. With every year, I am more and more appreciative of my siblings, Amy and Greg, and lifelong friends and colleagues who share my journey. Thanks to the Macatawa Group, XXceptional, Emerson Fellows, and the crews from High Street and El Dorado for laughs, love, learning together, and adventure.

In 2019, my wife Amanda and our children recognized that the implications of rapidly changing climate were resonating within me, and they have been unwavering in their support and belief in my calling to this new work. Amanda, you are my biggest champion, always supporting and encouraging me to be my best self. I am fortunate, indeed, to be sharing this "one precious life" with you. Maya and Theo, your sparks ignited this new path in my life, and I'm both grateful and deeply motivated to keep trying and working to engage others in this intergenerational, community endeavor. I love being your dad.

Finally, thank you to my parents, Jane and Larry, who modeled and set an expectation of being involved and engaged in the world. Although she is no longer with us, I know my mom would be standing shoulder to shoulder with me in this K–12 climate action movement, finding ways to contribute her energy and compassion.

FROM BOTH OF US

We are grateful for the many leaders who have welcomed us to this work and provided feedback and opportunities for learning and collaboration, including Sarah Bodor, Judy Braus, Karen Cowe, Kevin Coyle, Jim Elder, Andrea Falken, Mary Filardo, Sue Gander, Anisa Heming, Frank Niepold, Will Parish, Wendy Phileo, Sasha Pudelski, Jenny Seydel, Craig Schiller, Harley Stokes, Tish Tablan, Andra Yeghoian, and Elleka Yost.

We both owe a debt of gratitude to the team at Harvard Education Press, including Karen Adler for her insightful feedback and Jayne Fargnoli for bringing us on board. We are also grateful to Barrianne Brown for helping us get the book cleaned up for submission.

ABOUT THE AUTHORS

LAURA A. SCHIFTER, EDD, is a senior fellow with the Aspen Institute, where she founded and directs This Is Planet Ed, an initiative to unlock the power of education as a force for climate action, solutions, and environmental justice and to empower the rising generation to lead a sustainable, resilient, and equitable future. She is also a lecturer on education with the Harvard Graduate School of Education, where she teaches courses on education, climate change, and policy, and she serves on the Committee on Climate Education for Harvard University. She also serves as a member on the National Environmental Education Advisory Council with the US Environmental Protection Agency. Laura has published articles for *CNN*, the *Hechinger Report*, and *Education Week*, and her work with This Is Planet Ed has been featured in national media, including the *Washington Post*, *USA Today*, *NPR*, *ABC News*, and *The Hill*. Laura coauthored *How Did You Get Here? Students with Disabilities and Their Journeys to Harvard* and served as coeditor for *A Policy Reader in Universal Design for Learning*. She worked as a policy and research consultant with clients including Education 2020, the Massachusetts Department of Education, and the US Department of Justice. She also served as a senior education and disability adviser for Representative George Miller (D-CA) on the Committee on Education and Labor, an education fellow for Senator Chris Dodd (D-CT) on the Health, Education, Labor, and Pensions Committee, and was a fellow with the Century Foundation. After graduating from college, she taught elementary school in San Francisco. Laura earned an EdD in education policy, leadership, and instructional practice and an EdM in the mind, brain, and education from the Harvard Graduate School of Education, and a BA in American studies from Amherst College. Laura lives in Arlington, Virginia, with her husband and three daughters. In 2019, after years working in special education, Laura shifted her career to focus on the intersection of education and climate change.

JONATHAN KLEIN is cofounder and CEO of UndauntedK12, which supports America's public schools in making an equitable transition to zero carbon emissions while preparing our youth to build a sustainable future in a rapidly changing climate. His work at UndauntedK12 has been recognized with a fellowship from the Emerson Collective and the McNulty Prize Catalyst Fund. Jonathan has published articles for the *Los Angeles Times*, the *Hechinger Report*, *The Hill*, *The 74*, and the *Chronicle of Philanthropy*, and his work with UndauntedK12 has been featured in national media, including the *Los Angeles Times*, the *Boston Globe*, *NPR*, *Education Week*, and *Wired*. Jonathan has experience teaching, developing new schools, and working within large urban school districts, and he has led campaigns to change policy, elect equity-focused leaders, and generate hundreds of millions of dollars in new resources for children and public schools throughout the country. He is also a cofounder of GO Public Schools, Revolution Foods, and the Oakland Public Education Fund. He was chief program officer at the Rogers Family Foundation; special assistant to state administrators in Oakland Unified School District; Bay Area executive director of Teach for America; and an elementary school teacher in Compton, California. Jonathan received a BA in history from Yale University and an MBA from the University of California at Berkeley, where he also served on the faculty lecturing on nonprofit leadership and management. He is a credentialed California teacher and a member of the Aspen Global Leadership Network. Jonathan lives with his wife and two children in Oakland, California, where he coaches Little League baseball. He was radicalized around the climate crisis while chaperoning middle schoolers at one of the youth-led climate strikes in September 2019.

INDEX